STUDIES OF COMMUNISM IN TRANSITION

General Editor: Ronald J. Hill
*Professor of Comparative Government
and Fellow of Trinity College,
Dublin, Ireland*

Studies of Communism in Transition is an important series which applies academic analysis and clarity of thought to the recent traumatic events in eastern and central Europe. As many of the preconceptions of the past half century are cast aside, newly independent and autonomous sovereign states are being forced to address long-term, organic problems which had been suppressed by, or appeased within, the Communist system of rule.

The series is edited under the sponsorship of Lorton House, an independent charitable association which exists to promote the academic study of communism and related concepts.

Privatization in Eastern Europe

A Critical Approach

Iván Major
Senior Fellow
Institute of Economics
Hungarian Academy of Sciences

Edward Elgar

Published by
Edward Elgar Publishing Limited
Gower House
Croft Road
Aldershot
Hants GU11 3HR
England

Edward Elgar Publishing Company
Old Post Road
Brookfield
Vermont 05036
USA

British Library Cataloguing in Publication Data
Major, Iván
    Privatization in Eastern Europe: Critical
    Approach. – (Studies of Communism in
    Transition)
    I. Title II. Series
    338.0947

Library of Congress Cataloguing-in-Publication Data
Major, Iván
    Privatization in Eastern Europe: a critical approach / Iván
Major.
    176p. 22cm. — (Studies of communism in transition)
    Includes bibliographical references and index.
    1. Privatization—Europe, Eastern. 2. Europe, Eastern—Economic
policy—1989– I. Title. II. Series.
HD4140.7.M35   1993
338.947—dc20   93–24679
                                                CIP

ISBN 1 85278 887 9

Electronic typesetting by Lorton Hall

Printed and bound in Great Britain by
Hartnolls Limited, Bodmin, Cornwall

Contents

Tables

Preface

In parallel with the collapse of the communist political system in Eastern Europe and the former USSR, the privatization of state-owned property became the focus of discussion within and outside Eastern Europe. This was an obvious development since state-owned property accounted for 85–90 per cent of the national assets of the command economies. Private ownership and privatization, which had been taboo for East European economists during the communist era, surfaced as an immediate necessity in countries that aimed for an economic transformation from the command economy into a Western-type market economy with dominant private ownership. But the task of turning state-owned assets into privately-owned properties turned out to be overwhelming. It is perhaps one of the most challenging tasks of our time, both intellectually and in practical terms.

The articles and studies conducted on the subject by East European and Western economists and political scientists could fill whole libraries. Nevertheless, a comprehensive analysis of the issues and actual accomplishments of privatization in the East European countries does not yet exist. In fact, while hundreds or even thousands of articles and research papers have been written on East European privatization in great haste, only a few deeper studies have been carried out so far. János Kornai started a 'firework of ideas' with his book on *Indulatos röpirat a gazdasági átmenet ügyében* (A Passionate Pamphlet on the Cause of Economic Transition in Hungary) in 1989; an English edition of this book was published in 1990, under the title *The Road to a Free Economy*. Another, longer study conducted by David Lipton and Jeffrey Sachs (*Privatization in Eastern Europe: The Case of Poland*) followed Kornai's in 1990, and a third book was written by Olivier Blanchard, Rudiger Dornbusch, Paul Krugman, Richard Layard and Lawrence Summers: *Reform in Eastern Europe*, which appeared in the late summer of 1991. The latest effort is an ambitious project of the Central European University on East

ix

European privatizations, whose first reports, written by Roman Frydman, Andrzej Rapaczyński and John S. Earle and others: *The Privatization Process in Central Europe*, and *The Privatization Process in the Republics of the Former Soviet Union* are to be published in 1993.

The title of the present book refers to the works of the authors listed above. I intend to outline an approach to privatization in Eastern Europe that differs in substantial respects from those mentioned above. However, my approach is first and foremost a critique of the plans and programmes of the East European governments. Thus, I not only present various East European ideas and plans for privatization, but I comment those plans. In addition, I outline a new position on the principal issues of the privatization debate in Eastern Europe. Consequently, however neutral I had hoped to be in describing Eastern and Western views on privatization, this book is not a purely positivist contribution to our knowledge of the privatization experience of Eastern Europe. However, I have tried to indicate when I intend to provide a positivist analysis and where I am describing normative ideas.

I wrote this book during my stay as a visiting fellow at the Stockholm Institute of Soviet and East European Economics. I am deeply indebted to the whole staff of the institute for their unflagging help and assistance. I am grateful to the board of the institute and to Anders Åslund, its director, for their generous financial support. I benefited greatly from numerous discussions with Anders Åslund, Sten Luthman and Örjan Sjöberg on the complex issues and experiences of different East European countries with privatization. Sten Luthman and Georg Kjällgren also helped me with research materials on several East European countries. I also profited greatly from the discussions with Carlos Asilis, Igor Birman, Stuart Brown, Grigorii Khanin, Vasilii Selyunin and Tadeusz Kowalik, all visiting scholars of the institute during 1990–91. Kowalik also read and commented on the manuscript meticulously. In addition, he helped me with extensive information on the privatization programmes and actual experience in Poland.

A conference on Privatization in Eastern Europe, organized by the Swedish Employers' Confederation (SAF) and the Stockholm School of Economics on 2–4 October 1990, and a conference on Economics of Transition in Eastern Europe, organized by the *Oxford Review of Economic Policy* on 13–15 September 1991, also substantially contributed to my better understanding of the various issues of privatization. I am also grateful to Marion Cutting who helped to improve the language of this book.

After I returned to Hungary in 1992, I had the opportunity to discuss the manuscript with several Hungarian colleagues. Tamás Földi, István Csillag, Mihály Laki, Éva Voszka, Péter Mihályi, László Urbán and Pál Valentiny with their comments greatly helped me to improve and update the original study. I am also indebted to the series editor for his meticulous editorial work. Needless to say, any remaining errors are mine.

Iván Major

1. Introduction:
Analytical Framework

In 1989, successive political revolutions shook Eastern Europe.[1] The communist systems collapsed one after the other and by 1991 all the East European countries – from Albania to the USSR and its member republics – embarked on creating a market economy with dominant private ownership to replace their decaying command economies. Most of the experience of the time since then has been fairly disturbing, however. What started as a realization of long-awaited dreams by the peoples in Eastern Europe has been turning into a nightmare. After the abolition of the socialist political system, new – and, paradoxically as it may sound, democratically elected – authoritarian regimes, aggressive nationalism, anti-Semitism and a peculiar blend of modern and neo-feudal economic institutions are emerging. For many years it was the communist political system that proved to be the major obstacle to radical economic reforms in these countries. Now it seems that the greater than expected pains of the economic transformation and an ensuing renaissance of nationalism and populism constitute the most imminent threats to the new and fragile political democracies.

Politics and the economy were deeply intertwined under communist rule, and they have remained so under the new regimes, as well. More precisely, the new governing forces are using their political power to reinforce political control over and state intervention into the economy in order to enhance their power base. The institutions and methods of the government's control over the economy vary greatly among countries, since the level of political democracy and its stability are also different. However, the East European countries have

1 In this study the terms 'Eastern Europe' and 'East European countries' will denote Bulgaria, the former Czech and Slovak Federal Republic (ČSFR), the former German Democratic Republic (GDR), Hungary, Poland, Romania and the former Soviet Union. I shall mention Albania and Yugoslavia only occasionally.

one feature in common: the focus of power struggles and of economic transformation is the re-allocation of property rights, including, first of all, privatization of the state-owned property. Consequently, all the supportive arguments for privatization of state-owned property that are based on 'pure' economic rationality considerations, such as the gains in economic efficiency by privatization, or the superiority of private ownership over state ownership as regards flexibility, perpetual innovation and technical progress, rank as secondary in the East European political debates. However relevant these arguments are, they fail to address the most burning issues of the current East European economic transformations. In particular, these approaches do not indicate who can acquire the properties and who cannot and in what ways, that is, who will be the winners and who will be the losers in the redistribution of property rights.

This book considers the issues of privatization from this angle – that is, from the perspective of power redistribution – as well as the economic viewpoint. More than two years have passed since economic transformation started in several East European countries, which allows us to assess its accomplishments so far and to venture to forecast its future prospects. On the other hand, privatization is still in its initial stage in each country, that is, it is in the phase of the elaboration of competing blueprints for privatization rather than that of real action, which makes it important to examine and compare the most important proposals for privatization, too.

Apart from privatization, the economic transition of the East European countries requires the tackling of several other very complex tasks. The most important of these tasks are: stabilizing the crisis-ridden economies, creating the basic institutions of a market and liberalizing the economy, and restructuring industrial enterprises and other economic organizations. This study will focus exclusively on privatization and restructuring, and it will discuss the other areas of the transition only in connection with privatization and restructuring.

Besides privatization of the state-owned property, the birth and expansion of the private sector – that is, the creation of thousands of new private businesses – is also a decisive trend of the emerging market economies in Eastern Europe. Some East European economists even assert that dominant private ownership will be, first of all, the result of the spread of new private ventures, rather than that of the conversion of state-owned enterprises into privately-owned companies. Thus, the 'private economy' emerges beside the crumbling state sector rather than replacing the latter. I do not share this view. However important the mushrooming of the new private businesses, they are unable to attain a breakthrough in the demolition of the centrally-regulated economy. Privatization of the state-owned assets is important because this process is an organic part of replacing the command economy's infrastructure of political regulation by the infrastructure of a market economy. In this study, I shall focus exclusively on privatization and I shall not discuss the role of new private business in the transformation process.

My intention is to address the general issues of privatization of a former command economy rather than to analyse the technical details of concrete cases of privatization in the different countries. Nevertheless, I shall present the different approaches and the actual results of privatization in some East European countries: the former Czech and Slovak Federal Republic (ČSFR), Eastern Germany, Hungary and Poland. I shall also briefly outline other plans for privatization, namely those that have emerged in Albania, Bulgaria, Romania and the former USSR. The individual countries and cases will serve more as examples rather than as an exhaustive progress report on the privatization process in all East European countries.

Privatization in Eastern Europe is a very complex process that can be assessed on several levels. On the supply side, concerning what kind of properties are to be privatized, there seems to be a general consensus among economists and politicians that it is sensible to make a distinction among small-sized industrial and service companies, medium-sized enterprises, large state-owned enterprises, agricultural land properties, state-owned apartments and public utilities. It is more difficult to give an unambiguous listing of the demand side, by identifying what groups can be the potential new owners of the types of properties that are to be privatized.[2]

A possible approach distinguishes between domestic and foreign owners, and a second distinction can be made between the original owners of properties – when the demand will meet supply via reprivatization – and new owners. The group of new owners can be

2 Another terminology applies the terms 'input side' and 'output side' of privatization in ways similar to my use of the notions of 'demand side' and 'supply side'.

limited to those who will actually buy the properties for an effective market price, or it can be extended to include other groups of the population by using different techniques of free distribution or sales at discounted prices.

The definitions of supply and demand for privatization – which themselves depend on political and legal considerations, besides economic factors – have a decisive influence on how privatization can be accomplished. The standard methods of auctioning off properties – the case-by-case initial public offering or an outright sale of a given property to a selected buyer – are extensively discussed and known in the Western literature as well. Consequently, we do not need to deal with these techniques in detail, although a brief overview will be in order, focusing chiefly on the particularities of the embryonic East European capital markets that may require a modification of the standard methods. However, it is the new techniques – especially free distribution of properties combined with effective corporate governance – that deserve the most attention.

Since 1989, several East European and Western authors have formulated their proposals for the free distribution of a substantial part of the state-owned assets to the population at large. The advocates of this method have argued extensively for this solution, but they only hinted at how free distribution might be accomplished in practice, without bringing about complete chaos in the area of property rights and enterprise activities. In this study, I shall concentrate on the practical issues and the medium- to long-term aspects of privatization with free distribution of assets. Hence, most attention will be devoted to the process of conversion of property rights from the state to the people. Moreover, I shall discuss extensively the issues of efficient management control and restructuring connected with privatization via free distribution.

The structure of this study is as follows: after outlining the analytical framework in this chapter, in the next chapter I briefly describe the legacy of the command economy as regards political regulation of the economy, property rights and the structure of the national assets in the East European countries. In Chapter 3, I discuss the starting conditions and the most important tasks of the economic transformation that East European countries must face. In Chapter 4, I outline the main reasons – both economic and political – for privatization in Eastern Europe that are widely shared among economists in East and West. Then I confront those reasons with the actual arguments for privatization that emerged within the influential political groups of the East European countries during the initial phase of the political and economic transformation.

The different plans for privatization and restructuring that the individual countries accepted during the past three years are presented in Chapter 5. Next, I compare the actual results of privatization in four countries – the former ČSFR, the former GDR, Hungary and Poland – with the targets set by their governments. In Chapter 6, I discuss the different possible approaches to privatization. I briefly outline the proposals and blueprints elaborated mostly by Western economists, among them Anders Åslund, Olivier Blanchard and Richard Layard, and Jeffrey Sachs, which call for free distribution of state-owned properties. I focus on privatization with free distribution from several viewpoints. Specifically, I address the issues of social justice, speed, technical arrangements, and the potential longer-term effects of free distribution of property. The emphasis will be placed on the efficiency of management control ('corporate governance'), on the impact on restructuring, and on the emerging capital markets in Eastern Europe. I shall also try to assess the impact of free distribution on stabilization policy, or more concretely on inflation and money circulation in the economies in transition. Chapter 7 ends the study with concluding remarks.

The methods used in the analysis need some comment and qualification. A systematic account of privatization in all East European countries is still lacking. Consequently, most information comes from media sources and from different government documents published in the countries concerned. However, information on the same 'facts' from different sources is frequently contradictory and there is no way, or there are only very limited opportunities, to check its validity. This can be partly explained by the speed of the changes occurring in Eastern Europe. But in part the unreliability of information is due to the fact that the old information networks of the East European countries have disintegrated, but no new information system has yet been developed.

It is in the area of statistical data, especially, that information on privatization and the newly emerging private sector is the most scattered and unreliable. The old statistics system was created for the purposes of central control and regulation of the economy and it was based on the reporting obligation of state-owned enterprises. This system is unable to serve the needs of an economy with less regulation and with extensive liberalization. Hence, the old system was abolished but a new one has been unable to emerge so far. We do not possess credible figures for the GDP, foreign trade, producer and consumer price indices of the East European countries. Thus it is no wonder that we know even less about the myriad private initiatives that may result in the creation of new private companies. Therefore, statistical accounts of privatization must be handled with caution. Whenever possible, I shall point out the possible dangers of misunderstanding or misinterpretation of the data published about East European privatization measures.

2. The Legacy of the Command Economy

There is a consensus among analysts of the command economies, that

> The basic institutions of socialism in a Soviet-type economy are: (i) state ownership in productive assets, (ii) central planning of resources, and (iii) one-party political monopoly. Those institutions set the Soviet-type economy apart from other social systems.[1]

It is widely accepted by economists, too, that institutions rather than economic policy or quantitative changes in the economic processes are the most decisive factors in the performance of command economies. However, the interpretation of the command economy's three basic institutions mentioned above is far from self-evident. For instance, Pejovich himself points out that state ownership in practice means that all property rights of the state are concentrated in the hands of the Politburo of the communist party. This is an oversimplification of property rights in a Soviet-type economy. If it were true – as I believe it is not – this would mean that state ownership does not exist in reality in a command economy: it would be more a case of 'clan ownership' rather than state ownership.

In addition, several economists consider central planning of resource allocation as the *differentia specifica* of the command economy.[2] However, as was shown by Berliner (1957), Grossman (1983), Soós (1986a) and Major (1991a), central planning is only one – and not even the most important – of the regulatory devices applied by East European political and economic leaderships to achieve their pre-set targets. Moreover, it is completely misleading to describe central planning as a one-way vertical system of transferring orders

---

1 Pejovich (1990), p.97.
2 See, for example, Pejovich (1990), Kornai (1980), and Bauer (1981).

'from above' to lower levels of the economic organizations, where economic agents 'below' are only passive executives of the orders received from above.[3] Instead, central planning is a complex 'game' of summing up and breaking down physical and financial input and output targets for economic organizations at different levels, and a frequent modification of those targets, when each economic actor attempts to influence the final outcome of the planning process. This is not to say that members of the Politburo and managers of the enterprises were equal in power and economic influence. However, what the Politburo endorsed as its plan has almost always been a compromise among different pressure groups of the economy. As the command economy 'matured' and became more and more complex, the top-level political bodies were forced to form coalitions with managers of the largest enterprises.[4]

Finally, the monopoly position of the communist party meant much more than the omnipotent power of the party's Politburo. It resulted in all-embracing political regulation of the economy that was meant to serve as a substitute for the regulation by the market. In a later section I shall briefly outline the most important mechanisms of this political regulation,[5] but first, I shall describe the actual forms and operation of state ownership in the Soviet-type economy.

2.1 STATE OWNERSHIP, 'POLITBURO OWNERSHIP' OR '*NOMENKLATURA* OWNERSHIP'?

One of the first measures taken by the communist parties after they seized power was to 'nationalize' the bulk of privately-owned properties, including industrial companies, mines, banks, apartment buildings, service companies and agricultural land. The property rights of the nationalized assets were delegated to the state. However, 'the state' turned out to be an obscure, hardly applicable notion in a Soviet-type system. Although constitutions of the socialist countries formally existed – the Stalin version of the Soviet constitution was

3 Pejovich (1990), p.105.
4 See, for example, Szalai (1990), Åslund (1989), and Murrell and Olson (1991).
5 For a detailed description of the political regulation in a command economy see Major (1991a), Chapters 6 and 7.

adopted in 1936, and the constitutions of the other East European countries between 1948 and 1950 – those constitutions all encompassed at least one clause that made the rights of all other subjects of the constitution uncertain and allowed for an unlimited extension of the rights of the communist party. Consequently a real constitution that would have been based on a general consensus and support of the population, and could constrain the state's – or rather the party's – interference in the economy, could not emerge.[6] Party leaderships asserted that the state institutions were directly subordinated to the interests of the working classes and they represented nothing but 'working-class interests'. In reality, state institutions and organizations represented their own vested interests at best, beside their official functions to serve as transmission belts between the party bodies and the bottom-level economic and social organizations. Consequently, the notion of the 'socialist state' could be interpreted as a special mutation of the 'predatory or exploitation theory of the state'.[7]

If the legitimacy and authority of every single state institution was vaguely defined, and consequently uncertain, how then can state ownership be interpreted, if it can be interpreted at all? In order to test the applicability of the term 'state ownership' for a command economy, we must define 'ownership' too.

2.1.1 Legal Approaches to Ownership

In an 'ideal' capitalist society, where economic actors perform as equal partners on markets, or in a society where the hierarchy of different social groups is transparent and clearly defined, ownership is, first of all, a legal concept. Thus, the definition of ownership specifies one's rights and obligations in connection with a certain object and to other subjects. Consequently, property rights are a matter of the civil code rather than that of sociology or political economy.

---

6 In other words, a constitution as defined by Brennan and Buchanan (1985) was irreconcilable with the command economy.
7 North (1981), p.21.

On the basis of the above assumptions, the definition of ownership given by Pejovich is a useful point of departure:

> The right of ownership contains the following four elements: (i) the right to use an asset (*usus*), (ii) the right to capture benefits from that asset (*usus fructus*), (iii) the right to change its form and substance (*abusus*), and (iv) the right to transfer all or some of the rights specified under (i), (ii) and (iii) to others at a mutually agreed upon price.[8]

Pejovich points out correctly that from a legal point of view, conditions (iii) and (iv) are the most crucial aspects of ownership. In a socialist economy, functions (i) and (ii), that is *usus* and *usus fructus*, were shared *ex ante* between enterprises and central authorities, although the actual division of rights to use an enterprise's assets or use the benefits from those assets has been frequently modified, while to exercise functions (iii) and (iv), enterprise managers always needed the approval of higher authorities or they were directly ordered by the central bodies to execute a certain modification or transfer of their fixed assets.

The ambiguity of the legal concept of property rights under socialism is the direct reflection of the confusion of those property rights in a command economy. Pejovich attempts to resolve this confusion by over-simplifying the right of ownership in a command economy. He asserts that it is the Politburo that *de jure* and *de facto* exercises all property rights. However, the ambiguity is not a new phenomenon at all. Soviet and other East European jurists have been struggling with the principles of civil law under socialism since the early 1920s.

The Soviet school of civil law represented another extreme from the one presented by Pejovich. While Pejovich tried to apply the conventional legal framework of property rights to the socialist economies, the most prominent representatives of the Soviet school of 'revolutionary law', such as Pashukanis, Joffe, Gintsburg and Venediktov – and many others – insisted that communism would rapidly abolish the need for a civil law, or it would destroy 'the bourgeois framework of property rights' and replace those property rights with the 'revolutionary law of the proletariat'. The Soviet legal

---

8   Pejovich (1990), p.28.

traditions penetrated the other East European countries, too, and they were the strongest in the former GDR.[9]

However eagerly Soviet and East European legal experts tried to reconcile political regulation with civil law and with legalized property rights in the command economy, lawlessness and the rule of law coexisted in the East European countries. As successive economic reforms strengthened the autonomy of enterprises, the command economy came somewhat closer to an economy with transparent legal institutions, but it never became an economy that would itself have been based on, and regulated by, those institutions. Consequently, a purely legal approach to property rights in a command economy concealed, rather than revealed, how property rights were really exercised in the East European countries.

2.1.2 Property Rights from the Perspective of the Political Economy

In the command economy, it was the distribution of power and the bargaining position of different power groups rather than a transparent legal framework that had a decisive impact on the *de facto* property rights. Consequently, a 'political economy approach' to property rights may be more useful than a formal legal–institutional approach.[10] Thus, our point of departure can be that the allocation of property rights has always been uncertain in the East European countries. Formal regulations – however normative they tried to be – almost always ended up as discretionary rules that were applied to individual cases.

A few examples for the discretionary regulations were mentioned in the previous section. As we saw, East European central authorities attempted to control different segments of the economy with different economic measures. This sharp distinction between different regulatory devices was best reflected in the fact that central authorities tried to use completely separate regulatory tools for the day-to-day input

9 A comprehensive summary of the Soviet legal school and its successors in other East European countries is given by Sárközy (1981).
10 I use the term 'political economy' in the sense used by Brennan and Buchanan (1985).

requirements of the enterprises and for investments. Central authorities were most 'obsessed' with the regulation of investments.[11]

Another area of the central authorities' concern was the organization and reorganization of enterprises. As regards reorganization, this occurred in successive campaigns that aimed to reorganize the enterprise sector as a whole, rather than change the structure of a single enterprise. Individual enterprises were rarely reorganized on the basis of the actual state of demand for and supply of its products.[12]

Above, I used the terms 'enterprise' and 'central authorities' with reference to the holders of property rights. However, this is a simplification of the actual distribution of such rights. If one asked which institution was the ultimate owner of enterprises, there could be no unambiguous answer. The property rights retained by the central authorities were allocated among several bodies. Branch ministries – and in the 1950s and early 1960s 'industrial directorates' – were the direct superiors of enterprises, but they were not completely free to decide on the use of enterprise assets; in addition, their authority changed over time. Nevertheless, they had to operate in accordance with so-called 'functional' bodies, such as the central planning department, the ministry of finance, the national bank and the office of material allocation and prices. Consequently, there was a peculiar 'division of labour' regarding who could exercise property rights. The guiding principles of this division were seldom connected to economic or bureaucratic rationality: rather they reflected the power position of a certain ruling body.

Different party organs at several levels were also *de facto* holders of property rights. Ultimately, they could veto the decisions of the planning bureaucracy, or they could impose their own decisions on enterprises. However, after a few initial years of brutal repression where the police force was used to implement decisions, party bodies

---

11 Brus (1972), Goldmann and Kouba (1967), Bauer (1981), Soós (1986a). Brus argued that control and regulation of investments should remain in the hands of the central planners even in a reformed socialist economy, for the market is incapable of reacting to non-market signals, or the market signals cannot reflect long-term technical or economic changes. On the other hand, Hungarian reformers argued that enterprise autonomy cannot be full-fledged without the extension of the rights to invest to the enterprises: see, for example, Tardos (1972).

12 On centralization and decentralization campaigns see, for example, Voszka (1984) and (1990).

usually tried to reach a consensus with both the enterprise managers and the central bureaucracy, rather than give orders. They had no choice in this matter since their legitimacy and power base depended exclusively on the loyalty of others who also possessed some influence in the economy.

So far, we have discussed the distribution of ownership rights among the different influential groups in the command economy, and neglected the obligations connected with the ownership of property. Ownership also implies costs, not simply benefits, related to the possession of an asset,[13] and it is the owner who must assume those costs. On this count, the title of ownership was even less clearly defined in the Soviet-type economies than were the rights of the owners. In a 'classical' command economy, the inputs and outputs of each enterprise are set and allocated centrally. Consequently, enterprises cannot be made responsible for the costs of their operation as long as they fully obey central plans. However, in reality, such a system never existed in the East European countries. It could not exist since there was always a gap between plans and results, because of the central planners' inability to foresee the future. Moreover, it was in fact in the interest of the enterprises to deviate from the input and output targets specified by central planners. In part, everyday reality of shortages forced enterprises to do so, since they could not obtain the necessary inputs to fulfil their output plans. But plans had to be fulfilled somehow, at any cost. In addition, enterprises sought ways to fulfil their plan targets with the least possible effort.

In reaction to enterprises' efforts to enhance the scope of their decision making, central planners tried to increase enterprises' economic responsibility for their production by extending so-called 'self-financing' obligations to the enterprises. Some forms of 'economic accountability' (in Russian *khozraschet*) existed in the command economies from the very early period onwards. Formally, enterprises were obliged to bear the costs of their production, but not those of investment. Later, especially in countries experimenting with economic reforms, 'self-financing' was extended to a certain part of investments, too. However, in practice, 'self-financing' did not mean the full financial responsibility of the enterprises. Enterprise losses were always covered by the state budget, either in the form of direct

13 Fisher (1923), p.27.

subsidies or by cheap loans, or by other indirect subsidies.[14] Consequently, the costs attached to the property rights were spread over the society as a whole, while access to the benefits remained largely limited to powerful social groups. This phenomenon may be called an 'inverse externality' effect directly related to the institutional structure of a command economy.

In conclusion, we may say that state ownership in the strict sense of the word did not exist in a command economy. We could not find any state or party institution – or any well-defined group of them – that could be considered an exclusive owner of property in the East European countries. What existed instead was a peculiar form of 'collective ownership', where the property rights of the co-owners were vaguely defined, but those rights rather were subject to the permanently changing power position of the owners.[15] Thus, party bodies, planning bureaucracies and enterprise managers shared the property rights among themselves, while the costs related to those property rights were distributed among the whole population. The institutions of property rights in Hungary were vividly described by Szalai as a system of 'interest inclusion': that is, those influential groups who were able to acquire representation in the highest party and governmental bodies also became the *de facto* co-owners of the country's property.[16] Olson and Murrell, along similar lines, drew a parallel between the theory of collective action and the reality of decentralization of power in the socialist countries.[17]

---

14 This phenomenon is called by Kornai the 'soft budget constraint' of enterprises: Kornai (1980). Soós pointed out correctly that the enterprises' budget constraint is not soft but uncertain in a command economy, especially in the reformed East European economies: Soós (1984).

15 In a recent study three Yugoslav authors, Ellerman, Vahcic and Petrin (1991) argued that it is more accurate to apply the notion of 'social ownership' instead of state ownership in the case of communist and post-communist countries (p.283). I believe that the term 'social ownership' is misleading for communist economies, even for Yugoslavia which has had the longest record in so-called 'workers' self-management', since it would imply equal and unlimited property rights of all social groups in those countries. However, as I tried to show, it was not the case in Eastern Europe. While the authors are correct in saying that East European countries had a system of 'ownership by no one', from this it does not follow that 'everyone' was a co-owner of property. A similar approach can be found in Branko Horvat's article (1991), although his conclusion greatly differs from that of the above authors.

16 Szalai (1990) and (1991).

17 Murrell and Olson (1991).

It seems more appropriate to call the peculiar form of ownership in the East European countries '*nomenklatura* ownership', instead of state ownership. The term '*nomenklatura*' is used here in a broader sense than usual. It stands not only for a certain group of people, who are 'listed' by the communist party bodies, but it also reflects a complex system of interrelated interests of influential political and economic agents. Members of the *nomenklatura* did not belong to that group as persons (although personal connections usually had an important share in the formation of the group), but as representatives of powerful interests. They did not even need to be members of the communist party, although they had to be accepted by the party leadership. What is more important, their specific endeavours were tolerated even by the highest party bodies as far as those goals could be reconciled with the endeavours of the party leadership. Hence, it was not exclusively the Politburo but a wider group of institutions and actors who were able to exercise property rights in the command economies.

It must be emphasized that the term '*nomenklatura*' does not stand for a homogeneous group of people in the East European countries, but those who can be included in that group all have a decisive amount of decision-making power. Consequently, low-level leaders of an enterprise, such as the leaders of a workshop within a company or the so-called 'branch leaders' in an agricultural cooperative – however important their role in executing the enterprise's plans – cannot be considered as members of the 'owners' *nomenklatura*'.

2.2 ECONOMIC REFORMS AND OWNERSHIP

Formal and *de facto* rights and regulations were frequently divergent in a Soviet-type economy.[18] In fact, in each East European country property rights were divided among different power groups. However, from a formal perspective, the division of ownership rights was illegal in most countries. According to the law, subordinates were always

18 The distinction between formal and *de facto* economic regulation in the Soviet economy was extensively discussed in Hewett (1988); the Hungarian case is presented in an excellent way by Kornai (1959) and Soós (1986a); for Czechoslovakia see, for example, Šík (1967).

obliged to obey the decisions of their superiors. The annual and five-year plans were formally announced as laws binding on each economic actor, but in reality, higher-level decisions and their execution were negotiable between the rulers and the ruled. The successive attempts at economic reform in several East European countries can be interpreted as attempts to bridge the gap between the absurdities of formal regulation and reality.

Economic reforms partly sanctioned what had been an extensive but illegal practice on the part of enterprises. In addition, they attempted to increase enterprises' autonomy further. Such reforms occurred in the former GDR in 1963, in Hungary in 1968 and in 1984–85, in Poland in the early 1970s, in 1982, and then in the late 1980s, and in the USSR in 1965 and after 1986. An economic reform similar to, or even more radical than, the Hungarian one was initiated in Czechoslovakia in 1967, but it was aborted after the invasion of the country by the Warsaw Pact troops.[19] These reforms never attacked the issues of property rights in an open way. 'State ownership' remained a taboo subject in the East European economies. Reform blueprints emphasized the central authorities' endeavours to clarify which rights and responsibilities belonged to the centre and which to the enterprises. For instance, the Hungarian reform of 1968 was launched in the hope that along with the extension of enterprise autonomy, the central authorities could control the macroeconomic processes in a more efficient way.[20] However, in practice, economic reforms transferred several property rights from the central authorities to the enterprises.[21] The abolition of mandatory central plans, the liberalization of prices, the enhancement of the enterprises' freedom to invest, and, above all, the creation of enterprise councils (or, as they were called in Poland, 'employees' councils') as autonomous ruling bodies of the companies all pointed in the direction of enterprise self-management and *de facto* enterprise 'self-ownership'. This happened in the most explicit way in Hungary, and also in Poland.

By a decree of the Central Committee of the Hungarian communist party in 1984, state-owned enterprises were divided into three groups.

19 A detailed description of economic reforms is given by Johnson (1989).
20 See, for example, Antal (1985).
21 See, for example, Eörsi (1968) and Sárközy (1986).

The largest group consisted of enterprises which were directed by an enterprise council. About 75 per cent of the 2,400 state-owned enterprises belonged to this group. Two-thirds of the members of an enterprise council were elected by the employees of the enterprise and one-third of them were appointed by the general manager, who was also elected by the council. The party and the supervising branch ministry had veto rights in the appointment of the general manager. In small-scale enterprises the general assembly of the enterprise exercised the rights of management directly. This body also elected the general manager of the company. Finally, a few hundred of the largest enterprises remained under the direct control of the supervising branch ministry.

The new forms of enterprise management considerably increased the autonomy and power of the enterprise managers, and also increased the influence of the company's employees.[22] General managers became more dependent on their own staff, while their dependence on central authorities weakened. Enterprise self-management was envisaged by employees and even by leading economists as the means to avoid the dysfunctions of state ownership.[23] As a consequence, enterprise managers were under permanent pressure from their own employees to increase wages, even in loss-making companies. In several enterprises, excessive wages were paid from the amortization fund: in other words, the companies were using up their fixed assets.

In Hungary, the increased autonomy of the enterprises also yielded some positive results, beside the drawbacks mentioned above, whereas in Poland, enterprise self-management did not result in a growing flexibility of the enterprises. What factors could explain the differences in enterprise behaviour in the two countries? In Hungary, the enhancement of the autonomy of enterprises took place alongside

22 The essence of the Hungarian organizational and ownership reform of 1984-85 was vividly described by Sárközy (1986).
23 See, for example, Bauer (1984) and Soós (1990). It is worth noting that enterprise self-management has had fairly deep roots in Hungary and also in Poland. For instance, the uprising in 1956 aimed at the liberation of the country from Soviet influence, but internally, its central goal was to give a controlling position over enterprises and other economic institutions to the newly created 'workers' councils'. In Poland, self-management was a main issue of the 1956 events, too, and it became a founding principle of *Solidarity* in 1980-81.

a gradual process of liberalization of prices and foreign trade that had started in 1968. Consequently, Hungarian managers were not merely given more freedom to exercise some of the property rights of their companies, but they were also exposed to forces of the market, especially to foreign competition and contacts. Thus, although these reforms could not radically change the essence of the socialist economy, the decades of advancing and retreating on economic reform served as a learning process for enterprise managers and also for the central economic bureaucracy, however slow that learning process has been. By the late 1980s, the Hungarian producer and consumer price systems no longer contained severe distortions. The bulk of subsidies were abolished, and 70 per cent of foreign trade transactions became liberalized. In addition, a non-negligible private sector emerged. In Poland, the introduction of partial self-management of the enterprises remained a more isolated change, without a parallel reform in other economic institutions. Consequently, enterprise managers could more easily abuse their increased autonomy, without being held responsible for the performance of their company. Especially after 1979, when the Polish economy was slipping deeper and deeper into recession and shortages were aggravated dramatically in every sector of the economy, central regulation became more and more extensive. Consequently, enterprises were step by step deprived of their limited autonomy.

According to Soviet sources, by the late 1980s enterprise managers had become *de facto* holders of property rights in the USSR also,[24] although decentralization and liberalization of the Soviet economy lagged far behind Hungary and Poland. The source of increased autonomy and power of Soviet managers was a rapid disintegration of the central bureaucracy rather than a comprehensive economic reform. The strongholds of orthodox command economy remained Romania, Bulgaria, the former GDR and Czechoslovakia. This does not mean that enterprise managers in these countries had no influence at all on central decisions, or that they were not an organic part of the decision-making process. The difference between them and reforming countries was chiefly that autonomous decision making by enterprise managers remained illegal in the former group of countries while it

24 Grigoriev (1991).

became legalized in the latter. However, this seemingly formal difference had tremendous consequences for the behaviour of enterprises and their managers.

When the adverse effects of a monolithic state ownership (or, more accurately, non-private ownership) became the issues of open discussion in the late 1980s, and a search for a way to alter the system of property rights – including privatization – in the East European countries ensued, the actual division of property rights appeared to be a major stumbling-block to any changes. For instance in Hungary, the Company Act and an Act on foreign direct investment, both adopted in 1988, and the Act on Enterprise Transformation of 1989, authorized enterprise managers to 'corporatize' (in Poland 'commercialize') their companies, that is, to convert the enterprise into a joint stock company, or a group of limited liability companies under the direction of a trust. Enterprises and state-owned commercial banks could also buy shares of other enterprises.[25] However, selling enterprises or parts of them to private buyers – domestic or foreign – was not a part of the managers' authority. Even the conversion of enterprises into joint stock companies occurred with the assistance or active guidance of the central authorities, not to mention the sale of enterprise assets to private buyers.[26] Conversion of state-owned enterprises into joint stock companies and limited liability companies was authorized by law in Poland in 1987.[27]

The period between 1988 and early 1990 can best be described as chaotic in the area of property rights in Hungary, and the same situation also arose in Poland, although somewhat later. The central authorities started to accept a partial privatization of state-owned assets on pragmatic grounds. 'Smelling the wind of change', enterprise managers rushed to convert their enterprises into limited liability companies or joint stock companies in order to solve the enterprises' liquidity crisis. They also looked for foreign investors who could buy a share of the enterprises' assets and inject new

25 The idea of institutional cross-ownership among state-owned enterprises, including holding companies, was first published by Tardos (1972). Tardos's intention at that time was to find more efficient forms of ownership within the socialist economic system, that is, maintaining the dominance of state ownership.

26 See, for example, Voszka (1991a).

27 Grosfeld (1990), p.147.

resources into the ailing companies. However, they could not conclude private deals without the approval of the central authorities. Different government officials also travelled around the world and offered Hungarian enterprises for sale to foreign investors. But these officials failed to consult enterprise managers about their intentions. An atmosphere of mutual distrust developed between enterprise managers and government authorities. In Poland, the Act on Privatization, adopted in July 1990, gave a *de facto* right of veto concerning privatization to the employees' councils and even more importantly to the trade unions.[28] As a consequence, enterprises and trade unions succeeded in blocking any attempts to sell enterprise assets to private investors. As a final result of confused property rights, nobody knew who could do what and how it should be done.

The lack of transparent and unambiguous property rights gave way to suspicious 'sweetheart' deals among managers of state-owned enterprises and between managers and foreign buyers. This was more characteristic of Poland,[29] but was also present in Hungary.[30] As the political transition progressed in these countries, voices became louder and louder against the 'spontaneous privatization' of state-owned enterprises by enterprise managers (see below). In an atmosphere of total confusion and political attacks upon any attempt at privatization, governments simply chose to recentralize the previously decentralized property rights. New state bodies were created in almost every East European country to exercise the property rights of the state. Finally, 'real' state ownership was established in order to start the genuine privatization of state-owned assets. However sensible this solution seemed, it had several adverse effects on privatization when privatization began in earnest. The reasons for this 'backfire' effect can be traced back to the role of the party and state bureaucracies in the regulation of a command economy, and they will be discussed in the next section.

---

28 *Act on the Privatization of State-Owned Enterprises*, 13 July 1990 (Warsaw: Polish Interpress Agency).
29 See, for example, Grosfeld (1990), pp.147–9.
30 Tóth (1991).

2.3 POLITICAL REGULATION IN A COMMAND ECONOMY AND ITS CONSEQUENCES FOR PRIVATIZATION

With the abolition of private ownership and free markets, and the degradation of money to that of a more or less passive tool of accounting, the command economies were deprived of all the regulatory mechanisms that exist in a market economy. It was not only the nationalized companies and banks that found themselves in a vacuum, but the state authorities also lost the conventional devices of economic regulation. New methods of regulation had to be invented. An extremely detailed system of central planning, based on material balances and an expanding number of planning bureaucracies, was supposed to replace the economic institutions of capitalism.

However, throughout the decades of socialist economic history the formal rules and procedures of central planning had proved to be insufficient to regulate the command economies effectively and comprehensively. Central authorities needed additional levers in order to prevent the economy from developing imbalances on a catastrophic scale. A huge network of political regulation – using campaigns, coercion, and other 'non-traditional' methods – emerged, based on the party organizations, the trade unions and the mass media.[31]

Political regulation was meant to serve as a complementary network to the economic regulation provided by the planning bureaucracies. It was intended to be used under 'extraordinary' conditions when the usual planning procedures were too slow or too indecisive. But economic conditions almost always proved to be extraordinary in a command economy, since economic processes and interactions were deprived of any self-regulating mechanism. 'Polity' became unavoidably an organic component of 'economy'.[32] Perpetual political assistance came in the form of frequent coordination meetings among party economic officials, representatives of the supervising ministries and enterprise managers, and of political

---

31 The nature and practical application of campaigns is extensively discussed by Soós (1986b).
32 This observation contradicts Peter Wiles's statement (1982) that 'polity' must always be exogenous to 'economy'.

campaigns and permanent pressure on enterprise managers by the central authorities expressed as informal 'expectations' of the centre. Without this assistance, the command economies would have been unable to function. Consequently, political regulation soon became the decisive form of economic guidance, overshadowing the importance of central plans.

Political regulation of the economy was unable to perform 'fine-tuning', therefore it proved to be extremely inefficient and costly as a comprehensive system of regulation. However, political regulation was very effective in achieving relatively simple, one-dimensional goals, such as reducing the overall volume of imports of the enterprises or boosting investment outlays. Beyond these goals, to take into account and 'calibrate', for instance, the interrelated effects of different targets, simple in themselves, political regulation was not a feasible tool. Yet political regulation was not retained as a carefully applied device for special situations: instead, it became an all-embracing system of economic guidance. Party and state bureaucracies penetrated the enterprise sector deeply. Boundaries between the enterprises and the supervisory bodies became blurred. Enterprise managers obeyed the orders of party and government officials, since they were also representing the interests of their companies. On the other hand, party and government bureaucrats could pretend that they were running the industries as 'chief dispatchers'. The confused roles and responsibilities of supervisors and managers resulted in permanent mistrust and cheating between them, and a perpetual fight for control and autonomy on both sides. Central authorities and enterprises were both trapped in a 'double bind' relationship. This relationship could be considered one of the main factors behind permanently deteriorating economic efficiency and institutional efficiency of the command economies.[33]

Now, when the East European countries are starting to privatize state-owned properties, the entanglement of politics and economy must be taken into account as a crucial factor in the systemic changes. A modern market economy based on dominant private ownership cannot emerge until the system and institutions of political regulation are in place. Consequently, the new institutions of the East European

---

33 I discussed political regulation in a command economy in detail in Major (1991a); there I introduced the term 'institutional efficiency'.

states must have a clearly defined role to play in the process of transformation, a role that does not allow state interference in enterprise matters. As North phrased it, 'A theory of the state is essential because it is the state that specifies the property rights structure.'[34] Thus, the state has an increased responsibility to set the rules of the transformation of property rights. But it would be an unwarranted extension of this role if the state bureaucracy were to use its power to sell or distribute properties in its own political interests. As we shall see later, this danger is far from hypothetical. While tremendous attention is devoted to the 'false privatization' of state-owned enterprises by the old *nomenklatura* ('spontaneous privatization'), the attempts of the new political forces to use privatization in their own political and material interests are being somewhat neglected. If we do not address this danger we may soon witness a new *nomenklatura* emerging to replace the old one.

2.4 WHAT IS TO BE PRIVATIZED IN EASTERN EUROPE?

When the first programmes of privatization were launched in several East European countries in the late 1980s, economists had to face an immediate and enormous pitfall: nobody was able to tell what the 'true' value of the state-owned fixed assets was. Even the methods of how the evaluation of assets could be established were unknown. For four – in the former USSR for seven – decades, central statistical offices published only book values of the national assets. Without the existence of a capital market, and as a consequence of more or less arbitrary pricing, in a statistical system where tampering with the data served the vested interests of the central leadership and enterprise managers, those book values could tell little about the realistic market prices of assets.[35] In addition, information on the total material wealth of the East European countries, including agricultural land, forests, reserves of crude oil and other minerals, the housing stock and other

34 North (1981), p.17.
35 I discussed the problems of asset evaluation and the necessary distinction to be made between the book value and market price of capital in Major (1991b).

infrastructure, was scattered and even more unreliable than other indicators.

As regards the book value of fixed assets, only a few of the East European countries – such as Hungary and Poland – regularly published the net values of capital (that is, the value of assets without depreciation), while the others revealed only gross values.

There was no doubt about the fact that the state-owned property constituted the bulk of national assets in the East European countries. As the discussion on privatization heated up, more and more 'guesstimates' surfaced, which indicated that the share of state-owned property exceeded 85 per cent in each country, and it amounted to more than 90 per cent in some, such as in the former USSR, the former GDR, Romania and Bulgaria. Finally, each country started to publish data not only about the number of economic organizations, but on the companies' ownership and management structure as well. Official statistics have stressed the large share of state-owned enterprises, in order to demonstrate the magnitude of the problem of privatization. According to these data, the number of state-owned economic organizations that were possible candidates for privatization ranged between 2,400 in Hungary and 45,000 in the USSR.

Despite all the uncertainties related to the book value of assets, and notwithstanding the fact that book values had almost no relevance whatsoever to the market price of capital, these data have still occupied a major place in East European domestic discussions of privatization. East European politicians and economists, and especially those who were responsible for privatization, often compared the dubious book values of capital to the accumulated government debt of the countries concerned. They argued that the country's debt was incurred for the purpose of building up its capital stock: consequently, the sale of state-owned property must be used for the reduction of the debt.

If the state revenue has been a major aspect of privatization, it is worthwhile to give a brief account of the fixed assets of the East European countries as those assets were reported in the official statistics. A brief outline can provide us with a rough picture of the state-owned property's structure, too. In addition, asset values can be compared with the estimated magnitude of demand for properties, for example in the form of private savings and the inflow of direct foreign investment into the East European countries. If nothing else, a proof of the unfeasibility of a sensible privatization programme via sales based on book values may be worth the exercise. I shall proceed by examining individual countries, and give an overview on the whole group in a conclusion.

2.4.1 Czechoslovakia

The statistical yearbook reported only the gross values of capital. The gross value of fixed assets amounted in 1989 to about Kčs 4,500 bn in fixed, 1984 prices. Using the industrial price index for 1989,[36] the estimated value of fixed assets in current prices would increase to Kčs 4,550 bn. On the other hand, the statistical yearbook of 1990 gave a figure of Kčs 3,747 bn for the fixed assets in current prices in 1989 (p.238): that seems very unlikely. Applying a realistic exchange rate of Kčs 26 to one US dollar, the value of fixed assets amounted to $175 bn in 1989.

In 1989, the stock of the population's savings deposited in the savings bank amounted to Kčs 277.7 bn.[37] If we convert this amount into US dollars, using the exchange rate given above, the amount of savings would be equal to $10.7 bn, which is 6.1 per cent of the value of gross assets, and most probably less than 10 per cent of the value of net assets. The amount of foreign direct investment was negligible in 1989, and it started to grow only in 1991.

Table 2.1 shows the structure of fixed assets in 1989. As can be seen from the data, in 1989 about 34 per cent of the fixed assets was concentrated in industry and construction, 22 per cent belonged to material services and 31 per cent to non-material services and other branches; agriculture completed the distribution with more than 10 per cent of the assets. It is important to note that within the sector of non-material services, the housing sector took up 19 per cent of the country's total fixed assets. The housing stock consisted of 285,000 houses and 3,007,000 apartments of which 208,000 houses and 1,870,000 apartments were owned by the state.[38] The above groups of assets can be considered as candidates for different types of

---

36 *Statistické Prehledy*, 1991, No.9, p.275.
37 *Statisticka Rocenka 1990*, p.183.
38 Ibid., p.588.

Table 2.1 Fixed assets in Czechoslovakia (1989, in 1984 prices)

Gross fixed assets total (bn Kčs)	4,477
Share of sectors (in per cent)	
Industry	31.4
Agriculture	10.4
Construction	2.7
Water Management	4.5
Transport	13.1
Telecommunication	1.5
Domestic Trade	2.6
Foreign Trade	0.2
Housing	19.0
Communal	2.0
Education and Culture	4.4
Health and Social Welfare	2.0
Others	6.2

Source: _Statistická Ročenka 1990_, p.234.

privatization. To look at it from another angle, real estate and buildings constituted 71.1 per cent of the fixed assets, while the share of machinery, equipment and vehicles was 28.9 per cent.[39]

As regards the number of economic organizations, there were 8,856 registered, including 2,588 state-owned enterprises (with 2,019 employees on average) and 2,581 cooperatives (averaging 445 employees) at the end of 1989; the number of joint ventures with Western participation was negligible.[40]

Finally, if we try to assess the market value of the fixed assets in Czechoslovakia, a possible approach can be to take a share of the national income used as an estimate of gross profits produced in the whole economy. The used national income (in fixed 1984 prices) amounted to Kčs 575.6 bn in 1989. From this amount, Kčs 85.6 bn was used for capital formation, and Kčs 490 bn went to consumption. If we consider half of the consumption as wage costs – since 50 per cent of the population was actually employed in economic organizations – then the value of estimated profits would be Kčs 330.6 bn.

39 Ibid., p.25.
40 _Hospodarské Noviny_, 3 October 1991.

Consequently, the national average rate of profit would amount to 7 per cent (330.6 ÷ [4,477+245]). The rate of profit in a narrower sense – that is, relating the value of capital formation to fixed assets – would result in an even smaller rate of profit, namely, 4.2 per cent.[41] Considering the low level of profits and the necessary additional investments to restructure the country's fixed assets, the prospects for a sale of state-owned property on a mass scale were fairly dim in Czechoslovakia at the dawn of the economic transformation.

2.4.2 The Former GDR

In 1989, gross fixed assets amounted to M 1,745 bn (in fixed 1986 prices) in the GDR. According to the official statistics, industrial prices declined by almost 3 per cent between 1986 and 1989. Consequently, the value of fixed assets in current prices would have been M 1,696 bn. Using the exchange rate that was applied at the currency unification of the two Germanies (1:1, or 2:1 between the East German Mark and the DM) would provide us with a completely unrealistic picture. Even the exchange rate of 4:1, applied by East Germany before unification, would be unreal. It is more realistic to choose the rate derived from the cross exchange rates between the US dollar, the Hungarian forint and the East German Mark (9.3 Marks to one dollar). On that basis, the value of assets was $187.6 bn in the former GDR in 1989.

The savings deposits of the population amounted to M 159.7 bn.[42] The largest share of savings was converted into DM with an exchange rate of 2:1 to the DM. The total value of savings then equalled DM 79.9 bn, equivalent to $44.5 bn, which is 23.7 per cent of the value of fixed assets. The population's savings to fixed assets seems to be very impressive, but it would be misleading to consider savings as large as potential demand for properties. In consequence of the huge gap between East and West German wages and living standards, and because of the almost immediate jump in unemployment in the eastern part of Germany after unification, the bulk of private savings was not available for buying properties.

41 Data used for these calculations are from *Statisticka Rocenka 1990*, pp.21, 23, 137 and 220.
42 *Statistisches Jahrbuch der DDR 1990*, p.302.

Table 2.2 shows the sector distribution of fixed assets in the East German economy in 1989.

Table 2.2 Gross fixed assets in the former GDR (1989, in 1986 prices)

Gross fixed assets total (bn M)	1,745
Share of sectors (in per cent)	
Industry	46.1
Agriculture	10.1
Construction	1.7
Transport and Telecommunication	9.5
Domestic Trade	2.6
Foreign Trade	n.a
Housing	16.6
Communal	n.a
Education, Culture and Sport	3.9
Health and Social Welfare	1.6
Others	7.9

Source: Statistisches Jahrbuch der DDR 1990, pp.118–19.

Industry and construction accounted for almost 48 per cent of the assets in the GDR; material services had a share of 17 per cent, while the share of non-material services was about 25 per cent; agriculture accounted for 10.1 per cent of the assets. Within non-material services, the share occupied by housing was almost 17 per cent. The number of apartments amounted to 7,003,000 by the end of 1989. From this stock, 2,889,000 apartments were owned by the state, 1,230,000 by cooperatives and 2,883 apartments and houses were privately owned.[43] The share of real estate and other buildings was 60 per cent, while that of the equipment and vehicles was 40 per cent in the East German economy.[44]

The number of industrial enterprises was 3,374 (with 952 employees per enterprise on average); there were 16,475 enterprises in the construction industry, of which only 516 large enterprises were owned by the state (with 822 employees on average), while the

43 *Statistisches Jahrbuch der DDR 1990*, p.200.
44 Ibid., pp.118–20.

number of small private companies was 14,528 (with an average of 3 employees), and the rest belonged to the cooperative sector (with 55 employees on average). There were 3,844 agricultural cooperatives operating in the country, with an average membership of 240 persons.[45]

As regards the estimated market value of fixed assets, the calculated profit rate based on the value of national income used amounted to 8.3 per cent, while the rate of return on capital formation was 4.4 per cent in 1989.[46]

2.4.3 Hungary

At the end of 1988, in Hungary gross fixed assets amounted to HUF 4,691 bn, while the value of net assets was HUF 2,935.4 bn; the ratio of net to gross assets was thus 62.6 per cent. The Hungarian Statistical Office also published data on the country's 'reproducible national wealth'. This indicator included the amount of incomplete capital formation, and the stocks of raw materials, semi-finished products and consumer durables. 'Gross national wealth' amounted to HUF 5,659.3 bn in that year.[47] Applying the official exchange rate of the forint to the US dollar, the value of gross fixed assets was $72.1 bn, that of the net assets $45.2 bn, and national wealth amounted to $87.1 bn.

The population's savings deposits amounted to HUF 321 bn at the end of 1989, which when converted into US dollars equalled about $5 bn.[48] Of total savings, private savings in hard currency accounts were worth $400 m., or about 8 per cent of the total savings of the population. The ratio of private savings relative to gross fixed assets was 6.8 per cent, while the ratio of savings to net assets was 10.9 per cent. Taking into account that foreign direct investment increased to $550 million in Hungary up to the end of 1989, foreign investment and domestic private savings together still amounted to no more than 7.7 per cent of the value of gross fixed assets, or 12.3 per cent of net assets. The structure of gross fixed assets is shown in Table 2.3 below.

45 Ibid., pp.158, 192 and 212–13.
46 Ibid., pp.8, 15, 17 and 106.
47 *Statistical Yearbook 1989*, pp.92–5.
48 *Statistical Yearbook 1989*, p.19.

Table 2.3 Gross fixed assets in Hungary (1988, current prices)

	State, private and cooperative	Private and cooperative*
Gross fixed assets total (bn Forints)	4,691.0	1,334.7
Share of sectors (in per cent)		
Industry	23.8	30.7
Agriculture	9.6	2.4
Construction	1.3	..
Water management	5.4	..
Transport	16.5	3.9
Telecommunication	1.5	..
Internal trade	3.0	..
External trade	0.3	..
Personal and economic services (incl. housing)	28.5	63.0
Sanitary, social and cultural services	6.3	..
Administrative services	3.1	..
Others	0.9	..

* including industrial and trade cooperatives.

Source: Statistical Yearbook 1989, p.94.

As is shown in the table, industry and construction had a share of 25.1 per cent in gross fixed assets. Material services accounted for 26.4 per cent, and non-material and other services for 38.8 per cent of the assets. Agriculture ranked far behind with 9.6 per cent of the fixed assets. Within non-material services, housing took a substantial share in the state-owned and in the privately-owned assets as well. In the private and cooperative sector, privately-owned houses and flats accounted for 63 per cent of the properties. At the beginning of 1990, the number of apartments and houses was 3,842,000 in Hungary and among them some 800,000 were owned by the state (by local councils).

State-owned enterprises and incorporated economic companies

accounted for 51.7 per cent of gross fixed assets; the share of cooperatives was 7.9 per cent, while that of the small private organizations with legal entity was 0.9 per cent. Budgetary organizations and public utilities owned 19.8 per cent of the assets, while privately-owned apartments and houses had a 17.9 per cent share. Finally, privately-owned agricultural plots and properties of the self-employed added up to 1.8 per cent of total assets.[49]

The physical composition of gross fixed assets was as follows: real estate and other buildings accounted for 77.8 per cent, while machinery, equipment and vehicles constituted 22.2 per cent of the total assets. The number of state-owned enterprises, syndicates and trusts was 2,504 (with an average of 1,080 persons employed), and the number of agricultural and industrial cooperatives was 7,706 (with 234 employees on average) at the end of 1989. 307 joint stock companies and 4,485 limited liability companies existed in the country in 1989. The number of joint ventures with foreign participation was 1,250 with a total of $550 million foreign direct investment in the country.[50] The number of private businesses – including craftsmen – was around 50,000, but only 7.2 per cent of the labour force was legally employed in the private sector.

Finally, in an attempt to estimate the market value of fixed assets, I calculated the national rate of gross profit at 13.9 per cent, while the rate of return on capital formation was 7.2 per cent.[51] (However, the rate of net profit relative to fixed assets amounted to a mere 5.5 per cent.)

2.4.4 Poland

Poland's gross fixed assets amounted to Zl 106,000 bn in current prices, while the value of net fixed assets was Zl 59,000 bn in 1989, giving a ratio of net to gross fixed assets of 55.7 per cent. However, from the gross fixed assets, only Zl 81,700 bn was owned by the state, and the rest belonged to private owners. Using the official exchange rate of 9,500 Zloties to one US dollar, introduced on 1

---

49 *Statistical Yearbook 1989*, p.94.
50 Ibid., p.64, *Statisztikai Havi Közlemények*, 1991, No.4, p.64 and *MTI Econews*, 23 September 1991.
51 *Statistical Yearbook 1989*, pp.5-6, 10, 76, 94 and 98.

January 1990 as a major device of the Balcerowicz programme, and taking into account the increase in prices of investment goods of some 295 per cent in that year,[52] the estimated total value of gross fixed assets was $144.5 bn, while the value of the net fixed assets was $80.4 bn in 1989. The value of gross fixed assets amounted to $111.4 bn in the state sector.

The population's savings accounted for Zl 95,796 bn, of which private money stocks in hard currencies were worth of Zl 64,291 bn.[53] Converting private money stocks into dollars, the amount of savings was equal to $10.1 bn, or 7 per cent of gross fixed assets, and 12.6 per cent of net fixed assets. According to expert estimates, there was an additional $3-4 bn money stock held by the population in hard currencies, 'hidden under mattresses' or deposited in foreign banks. Calculating from this amount, the ratio of the private money stock to gross fixed assets would increase to 9.8 per cent, while that of the net assets grew to 17.5 per cent. However, other economists doubt that these figures are realistic. They argue that in 1989, when liberalization of private businesses started and private ventures boomed in Poland, no new money resources of the population appeared on the scene. (A group of British experts estimated a much smaller ratio of private savings to the state-owned assets, namely 1.5 per cent.)[54]

The structure of assets according to branches and according to forms of ownership is given in Table 2.4. As is shown in the table, 28.5 per cent of the gross fixed assets belonged to industry and construction, 21.6 per cent to material services and 27.4 per cent to non-material and other services. Housing and communal services alone accounted for about 20 per cent of the assets. Agriculture also had a fairly high share with 22.5 per cent. As regards the private sector, agricultural land and equipment constituted the bulk of the private property in 1989, while in addition, the housing sector also had a considerable weight. As regards the physical composition of assets, 75.5 per cent comprised real estate and buildings, while the share of machinery, equipment and vehicles amounted to 24.5 per cent.

At the end of 1989, the number of state enterprises was 7,337,

---

52 *Rocznik Statystyczny 1990*, p.183.
53 *Biuletyn Statystyczny*, Vol.XXXV (April 1991), Nos 1-3, p.33.
54 Tadeusz Kowalik (personal communication).

Table 2.4 Gross fixed assets in Poland (1989, current prices)

	State and private	Private
Gross fixed assets total		
(bn Zloties)	105,999.9	24,273.8
Share of sectors (in per cent)		
Industry	26.2	..
Agriculture	22.5	71.4
Construction	2.3	..
Transport1	8.9	4.2
Telecommunication	0.6	..
Trade	2.1	..
Housing and communal	20.2	24.4
Education, culture		
and sport	3.0	..
Health and social welfare	1.0	..
Others	3.2	..

Source: *Rocznik Statystyczny 1990*, pp.242-4.

employing 1,580 persons on average. Among them, 2,440 operated in industry, 1,542 in construction and 1,384 in agriculture. The number of joint stock companies and limited liability companies (*Spółki*) was only 340, while 429 joint ventures with foreign participation were established. The number of individual business establishments amounted to some 813,500.[55] Finally, the estimated profit rate (the part of the national income used relative to fixed assets and wage costs) amounted to 7.3 per cent, while the rate of return of capital formation - relative to gross fixed assets - was 3.1 per cent.[56]

2.4.5 The Former Soviet Union

National wealth (*natsional'noe bogatstvo*) of the USSR stood at R4,500 bn in 1990. Within national wealth, the value of gross fixed assets was R2,958 bn. Using the exchange rate of 15 roubles to one

55 *Biuletyn Statystyczny*, Vol.XXXV (April 1991), Nos 1-3, pp.26 and 57-8.
56 *Rocznik Statystyczny 1990*, pp.xxxiii, 125 and 244.

US dollar in 1990,[57] which was considered realistic by most Soviet economists, the value of national wealth was $300 bn, while that of fixed assets stood at $197.2 bn.

Private savings deposited in the national savings bank amounted to R380.7 bn in the USSR in the same year. This amount equalled $25.4 bn, or 12.9 per cent of the value of gross fixed assets. There are persistent rumours – shared by many Soviet economists – that an additional money stock of $4 bn to $10 bn is hiding in foreign bank accounts and in the pockets of the KGB and members of the so-called mafia. Were this true, the savings and money holdings of the population and mafia members would add up to almost 18 per cent of the country's gross fixed assets. Estimating the value of net assets as 60 per cent of the value of gross fixed assets – a plausible estimate based on data of other East European countries – legally deposited private savings would equal about 21.4 per cent of the net assets, while the ratio of the estimated legal and illegal money stocks to net assets would be almost 30 per cent. The structure of the assets is given in Table 2.5 below.

As can be seen, industry and construction took up 36.1 per cent of gross fixed assets; material services accounted for 17.8 per cent, and non-material services for 33.1 per cent of the assets. Within non-material services, the share occupied by housing was more than 18 per cent. The share of agricultural assets stood at 13 per cent. As regards the physical structure of assets, data are given only for the so-called 'productive' sectors: that is, these data exclude non-material services. In the productive sectors, the share of real estate and buildings was 60.2 per cent, while that of machinery, equipment and vehicles was 39.8 per cent. In the non-material services, the share of real estate can be estimated as 90 per cent: thus, the share of real estate and buildings in the whole Soviet economy can be estimated at around 70 per cent.

There is, of course, an immense diversity among member republics

57 This was an exchange rate estimated by some leading Soviet economists, such as Boris Fedorov, Grigorii Khanin, Yevgenii Yasin, Sergei Aleksashenko and Alexandr Shokhin, all participating at a conference on 'The Soviet Economy in Crisis and Transition' held in Stockholm, on 11–12 June 1991. Since then, the official exchange rate of the rouble has increased tremendously; the rate varied between 60 and 150 roubles per dollar in early 1992, and shot up to R350–400 per dollar by the end of the year; the rise continued spectacularly into 1993.

Table 2.5 Gross fixed assets in the former USSR (1990, fixed prices)

Gross fixed assets total (bn Rbl)	2,958

Share of sectors (in per cent)

Industry	32.6
Agriculture	13.0
Construction	3.5
Transport and telecommunication	14.0
Trade	3.8
Housing	18.2
Communal	4.6
Education and culture	4.1
Health and social welfare	6.2

Source: *SSSR v tsifrakh v 1990 godu*, p.48.

of the former USSR as regards the procurement of fixed assets. Consequently, a more detailed regional analysis of capital allocation and privatization would give a more accurate picture than the one based on data relating to the all-union level; however, such an analysis is beyond the scope of this study.[58]

The number of industrial enterprises was 45,000 (employing 787 persons on average) in 1990. Of these, 2,400 enterprises were 'leased out' to employees and managers (*arendnoe predpriyatie*), with 708 employees on average. The total number of leased companies stood at 6,200 with an average of 581 employees each. After industry, it was in retail trade and catering that most such companies (2,000) operated. The number of cooperatives exceeded 245,000, of which the number of agricultural cooperatives (*kolkhozy*) was 10,400. These cooperatives employed 25 persons on average, while the average employment in the *kolkhozy* was 1,077 persons.[59] Private activities - legally permitted only on an individual or family basis - were concentrated in small-scale services and agriculture. The number of farms leased by private persons accounted for about 40,000 in 1990, employing

58 Brown and Asilis (1991) have performed such a regional study for the former USSR.
59 A comprehensive study of the cooperative sector - as the main form of entrepreneurship in the former USSR - has been conducted by Slider (1991).

some 100,000 persons. The number of privately employed persons was 4.5 million,[60] or 3.3 per cent of total employment in the economy. The number of registered joint ventures with foreign participation was close to 1,000 in 1990; however, in reality most of these companies existed only on paper and they had no actual operation in the USSR at all. Western investors wanted to get into the Soviet market, but they found it extremely risky to take on a considerable exposure in the Soviet economy. (As could be seen, for example, in the former Prime Minister Pavlov's and the KGB's attacks on foreign companies and banks in the autumn of 1990, foreign investors had well-founded reasons for caution.)

In an attempt to estimate the market price of fixed assets I also calculated the national profit rate for the USSR. The rate of profit relative to wage costs and fixed assets stood at 13.6 per cent, while the rate of return on capital formation was 7.4 per cent.[61]

2.5 CONCLUSIONS

The conclusions that can be drawn from the above analysis are most striking. First, if we converted the total book value of gross fixed assets of the five East European countries discussed above into US dollars, those fixed assets would account for a mere 6.5 per cent of the annual aggregate real GDP of the United States, Canada, Japan and the European Community in 1989, or 14.9 per cent of the GDP of the United States alone.[62] If we take the former GDR separately and compare it to West Germany alone, the East German assets were worth 20 per cent of the West German GDP in 1989. In the same year the ratio of gross fixed assets of the four remaining countries was 4.9 per cent to the aggregate GDP of the developed countries, equal to 11.3 per cent of the US GDP, or 62.5 per cent of the West German GDP. Table 2.6 shows the amounts and ratios of private savings and gross fixed assets in the East European countries in a concise form, after conversion into US dollars.

60 *SSSR v tsifrakh v 1990 godu*, pp.63–8 and 204.
61 Ibid., pp.44, 73, 115 and 251.
62 I used the GNP data of 1989 as given in the *CIA Handbook of Economic Statistics, 1990*, p.30.

Table 2.6 Fixed assets and private savings in Eastern Europe in 1989 (in bn $)

	ČSFR	GDR	Hungary	Poland	USSR
Gross fixed assets (bn $US)	175.0	187.6	72.1	144.5	197.2
Private savings[a] (bn $US)	10.7	44.5	5.0	10.1	25.4
Savings : assets ratio[a] (per cent)	6.1	23.7	6.9	7.0	12.9
Private savings[b] (bn $US)	n.a.	n.a.	n.a.	14.1	32.4
Savings : assets ratio[b] (per cent)	n.a.	n.a.	n.a.	9.8	16.4

[a] official data on savings   [b] official plus estimated savings.

Sources: as in Tables 2.1–2.5.

Secondly, we found that savings and additional money stocks of the population, although not negligible, were quite insufficient to acquire a substantial share of the state-owned property in any East European country, if that property were sold at book-value prices. Even private savings and foreign direct investment added together could have bought only less than 20 per cent of the state-owned property in the individual countries. (East Germany is a special case here because of the currency unification of the two Germanies.) We could also observe great variation among countries as regards the potential purchasing power of the population against properties. It is somewhat surprising that Poland ranked far behind the other East European countries in this respect, despite the commonly-held beliefs that Poles have been the most skilful in trading on the semi-legal or illegal 'CMEA[63] street markets' and in Western cities too. On the other hand, data on undeposited private money stocks or deposits in foreign banks in hard currencies are very unreliable, and these data can substantially modify the picture given of private savings in the different East European countries.

63 CMEA: Council for Mutual Economic Assistance, now defunct.

Thirdly, as was shown above, the general rate of profit, or the rate of return on capital formation, was fairly low in each East European country. Of course, overall figures do not indicate that each state-owned enterprise worked with very low profitability, or that the market value of any individual enterprise must be near to zero or negative. However, it is equally true that, for an economy as a whole, it would be unrealistic to expect a substantial amount of new investment to come when the prospects of profitability are highly uncertain.

Since 1989, considerable changes have occurred regarding private savings and also the value of state-owned enterprises in all East European countries. Concerning savings, a trend towards an increase can be observed in several countries, which is an obvious consequence of the populations' growing uncertainty. On the other hand, the amount of private savings is, to some extent, a mystery for analysts, for the economies are in a deep recession and the number of unemployed is growing very fast. For instance in Hungary, the amount of private savings was around HUF 800 bn, or 11.5 per cent of the GDP in mid-1992, and it rose to HUF 1,050 bn or 13 per cent of the GDP by the end of the year. But nobody could really tell how large a share of this amount was deposited in Hungarian banks by foreigners (among others, by citizens of the disintegrating Yugoslavia and by undetectable sources). Most economists in these countries consider a sizeable share of private savings as 'hot money' that cannot be taken into account as a solid factor of demand for state-owned properties.

Another striking phenomenon of the past three years has been that most state-owned enterprises have permanently lost value. This was partly due to the complete collapse of the CMEA trading system, entailing the heavy loss of markets for most companies. However, the value of state-owned enterprises was also reduced by their own desperate effort to avoid bankruptcy: notably, enterprises sold their assets for cash and they paid wages from depreciation, simply in order to stay afloat.

As a consequence of growing private savings and decreasing asset values of the state-owned enterprises, the ratio of savings to asset values has increased in the East European countries since 1989. Theoretically, thisshwould have improved the population's position in acquiring property. However, in practice almost nothing happened in the countries concerned to mobilize private savings. Hungary was perhaps the only country where the national bank and also the commercial banks offered lucrative bonds and other securities to the population, but even in that country, accumulated bank deposits were returned to private investors or entrepreneurs to only a very limited extent. Private savings were used to finance the governments' deficit instead. Hence, the slow process of privatization simply further decreased the value of state-owned enterprises and it maintained the companies' low profitability, which aggravated the prospects for future privatization as well.

At the same time, another extreme must also be avoided. A sizeable group of respected economists in East and West argued that the real market value of the state-owned property in Eastern Europe was nil or even negative. Olivier Blanchard and Richard Layard, Jeffrey Sachs, Lawrence Summers and Anders Åslund may be mentioned as the most ardent advocates of this view; a most insistent supporter of this idea was the Czechoslovak Finance Minister, later Prime Minister, Václav Klaus, among other East European economists. A consequence of that view is that all properties should be offered free of charge to anyone who is willing to acquire and utilize those properties. This approach cannot be supported by the facts, however. We observed that real estate and buildings constitute about 70 per cent of fixed assets in all East European countries. If we accepted that accumulated machinery and equipment can best be used as scrap – a proposition that is very close to reality – the bulk of properties would still have a non-negligible positive value. This assertion is backed by evidence of immense price increases of real estate and land in those countries. It is reasonable to say that the existing stock of real estate needs a considerable amount of investment in order to upgrade and modernize the properties. The required additional investments would obviously reduce the present value of the properties' market price, but those investments would increase the future value of properties. Consequently, the 'lack of real value' of the state-owned property is not a strong argument for free distribution of assets.

Fourthly, several thousand state-owned enterprises existed in each country, mostly in industry and in public services. The number of state-owned enterprises per one million employees ranged between 400 and 500 in each East European country. Consequently, privatization and restructuring of these enterprises called for new, unconventional methods, other than attempting to transform the structure and ownership of each company separately, by the state administration. The need for inventive solutions of privatization was further underlined by the fact that the conventional institutions and devices of a Western-style capital market were non-existent, or barely existed, in the East European countries. For instance, the number of joint stock companies started to grow in each country in the late 1980s, but a stock market had not yet been created, and the banking sector was underdeveloped. Thus, the existing commercial banks were not able to tackle the problems of asset management.

At the same time, the organizational structure of the industrial enterprise sector and agricultural production allowed for the application of relatively simple methods in privatization. In those sectors, most of the state-owned enterprises consisted of a large number – not infrequently even hundreds – of more or less separate production or service units. Thus, a swift decentralization along the natural boundaries of autonomous factories or retail trade shops made it feasible to auction off or lease out thousands of smaller companies to new private entrepreneurs. The bulk of assets of the agricultural cooperatives could easily have been transformed into private property, to be owned by the members of the cooperatives. This would simply have needed the distribution of the cooperatives' assets among their members, according to their former contribution to the cooperative's property in land and other assets, and according to the length of the members' employment. Apartments owned by the state could have been sold relatively easily to the tenants at a discounted price, or they could have been offered to outside investors for a realistic market price that already existed in several East European countries.

It was a relatively small but concentrated group of the very largest state-owned enterprises, and in addition a few huge service monopolies, that would have needed an approach completely different from the methods mentioned above. However, in reality, the process of transforming state-owned property into privately-owned assets proved to be much more complex and cumbersome for all kinds of properties in each East European country than would have been suggested by the 'ideal scenario' outlined above. Why is this so? We attempt to answer this question in the following chapters.

3. Starting Conditions and Issues in the Economic Transformation

There is no need to elaborate in detail on the fact that since the late 1980s all East European countries have witnessed the most severe economic crisis of their socialist history. In some cases, such as Bulgaria, Romania and the former USSR, the crisis even turned into an economic disaster.[1] In fact, the decay of the command economies – besides the 'Gorbachev factor' and a political 'domino effect' among the East European countries – largely contributed to the collapse of the communist system in Eastern Europe. But the very same economic factors that helped new political systems emerge also constituted extremely unfavourable conditions for the establishment of political democracy and for the economic transformation (see data in Table 3.1 below).

The immediate and most visible symptoms of the crisis were the domestic and external financial imbalances in these countries. External convertible currency debt accumulated rapidly during the late 1980s and early 1990s in most countries. (An exception so far has been Czechoslovakia.) Bulgaria, Poland, Romania and the former USSR became, in reality, insolvent, although only Bulgaria and Poland formally rescheduled their debt repayment obligations. In addition, the deficit of the state budget surged in the East European countries, contributing greatly to the acceleration of inflation. Finally, money and monetary policy started to play a decisive role – however peculiar – in the economic policy of the command economies.

Paradoxical as it may seem, the most visible phenomena of an economic crisis – and the economic issues that concerned East European central authorities the most – were those financial indicators

---

1 Literature on the subject abounds: see, for example, Joint Economic Committee (1989), Johnson (1989), Dembinski (1991), Khanin (1991) and Major (1991a).

Table 3.1 Annual change of selected economic indicators of the East European countries, 1987–91 (in per cent, if not stated otherwise)

	1987	1988	1989	1990	1991[a]
Bulgaria					
GNP	-1.0	0.9	-0.1	-13.6	-15.0
NMP	5.1	6.2	-0.4	-11.5	-20.0
GI[b]	7.3	3.9	-7.7	-11.4	19.0
CPI	2.7	2.4	6.4	70.0	550.0
Unemployment	..	..	..	1.9	10.5
SBB/NMP	0.6	-2.0	-0.7	-9.5	-4.0[c]
BFT, bn $	-0.9	-1.0	-1.2	-0.8	-1.5
DSR	64.0	58.0	74.0	122.0	..
Czechoslovakia					
GNP	1.1	1.8	1.0	-1.0	-16.0
NMP	2.1	2.3	0.9	-1.2	-18.0
GI	4.4	3.1	1.6	2.3	..
CPI	0.1	0.2	1.4	18.4	60.0
Unemployment	..	..	..	1.0	8.0
SBB/NMP	-0.1	-0.1	-1.1	-5.0	0.0
BFT, m. $	-144.0	-89.0	287.0	-450.0	-200.0
DSR	27.0	22.0	28.0	28.0	30.0
GDR					
GNP	1.7	1.1	1.2	-12.6	-21.5
NMP	3.6	2.8	2.0	..	..
GI	8.0	8.2	-1.0	-5.7	10.0
CPI	0.0	0.0	2.0	..	..
Unemployment	..	..	..	2.5	12.3
				8.6[d]	26.1[d]
SBB/NMP	0.1	0.1	..	-12.5[e]	-4.7[e]
BFT, m. $	448.0	-952.0	-857.0	-1084.0[f]	1202.0[f]
Hungary					
GDP	4.1	-0.1	-0.2	-5.0	-10.0
NMP	4.1	-0.5	-1.1	-5.5	-9.0
GI	11.0	-8.3	3.9	-9.0	-15.0
CPI	8.6	15.5	17.0	29.0	35.2
Unemployment	..	..	0.4	1.5	7.5
SBB/GDP	-2.8	-0.7	-2.9	0.0	-3.0
BFT, m. $	-370.0	538.0	540.0	945.0	-350.0
DSR	62.0	59.6	52.0	51.8	40.0

	1987	*1988*	*1989*	*1990*	*1991ᵃ*
Poland					
GDP	2.0	4.7	0.5	-12.0	-12.6
NMP	1.9	4.9	0.3	-13.0	-13.0
GI	4.2	5.4	-2.3	-8.0	-9.4
CPI	25.3	61.3	237.9	684.3	70.0
Unemployment	..	..	0.0	6.5	11.8
SBB/GDP	..	..	-4.4	1.0	-5.0
BFT, bn $	1.23	1.01	0.77	3.80	0.0
DSR	79.0	68.0	76.0	71.0	..
Romania					
GNP	-0.8	1.7	-1.5	-7.0	-10.0
NMP	0.8	-0.8	-10.9	-10.5	..
GI	0.9	-1.3	-1.8	-35.0	-20.0
CPI	0.5	0.5	1.1	5.7	200.0
Unemployment	..	..	..	0.0	2.5
BFT, bn $	2.80	3.55	2.52	-2.82	-1.5
DSR	79.0	68.0	76.0	71.0	..
USSR					
GNP	2.9	5.5	3.0	-2.0	-14.0
NMP	1.6	4.4	2.4	-4.0	-16.0
GI	5.6	6.2	4.7	-2.5	-9.0
CPI	1.3	0.6	2.0	5.3	100.0
SBS/GDP	-6.3	-9.3	-8.8	-20.0	-27.0
BFT, bn $	8.43	4.22	-1.54	-0.74	0.0
DSR	24.0	22.0	26.0	29.0	..

Notes: GNP=Gross National Product, GDP=Gross Domestic Product, NMP=Net Material Product, GI=Gross investments, CPI=Consumer Price Index, SBB=State budget balance, BFT=Balance of foreign trade, DSR=Debt service ratio.

ᵃ preliminary; ᵇ in nominal value; ᶜ first ten months of the year; ᵈ rate of part-time employed; ᵉ budget balance relative to GNP; ᶠ only industrialized countries.

Sources: *CIA Handbook of Economic Statistics 1990*, p.39, *Östekonomisk Rapport*, No.2, Vol.3, 25 March 1991, No.5, Vol.3, 1 June 1991, No.8, Vol.3, 21 October 1991, *PlanEcon Report*, Vol. VI, Nos 18-19, p.4, No.25, p.2, Nos 36-7, p.4, Vol. VII, Nos 13-14, p.2, Nos 32-3, p.2, Nos 34-5, pp.9, 19-20, *Financial Market Trends*, OECD, February 1991, p.26, *Hospodarské Noviny*, 4 September 1991, *Statistická ročenka 1990*, pp.139 and 152, *Statistisches Jahrbuch der DDR 1990*, pp.101 and 299, *Statistical Yearbook of Hungary 1989*, pp.78-9, 98, 307, *Życie Gospodarcze*, 13 October 1991, *ECE Economic Survey of Europe in 1990–1991, DIW Wochenbericht*, Nos 26-7 (27 June 1991), and 33 (15 August 1991); *Országos Munkaügyi Központ Jelentései*, Budapest, 1992.

that had been considered the least important attributes of a command economy. In fact, there have been signs of a swing to the other extreme. Thus, while heavily emphasizing the danger of financial instability and the consequent need for a stabilization programme, many economists started to 'forget' (or did not fully grasp) that the economic crisis of the command economies was, above all, structural and institutional in nature. Hence, low-level economic and institutional efficiencies and an in-built (that is, systemic) inflexibility of the centrally-regulated economies were at the core of their economic collapse. This is not to say, by any means, that tackling an acute financial disaster can be pushed aside or postponed: measures aimed at stabilization must come first in an economy that aspires to comprehensive economic transformation. In particular, an extremely high rate of inflation, fuelled chiefly by irresponsible government spending, must be curbed. However, it should always be kept in mind that financial imbalances constituted a 'lethal' danger not in themselves, but because they were maintained and fuelled by a disintegrating economy, declining national product, plunging foreign trade, a rapidly growing number of bankrupt enterprises and an upsurge in unemployment.

As Table 3.1 demonstrates, the overall picture on the East European economies looks fairly gloomy, with a definite downward trend in each country. National product and investment are plunging (the only exception may be Eastern Germany for 1991). Contracting production and declining investment allow little room for macroeconomic adjustment and structural changes without huge sacrifices. A major factor behind the economic crisis of the East European countries is an almost total collapse of foreign trade among the former member countries of the CMEA. After shifting their payment arrangement to convertible currencies on 1 January 1991, the six CMEA member countries' exports to and imports from the former USSR dropped by 35–65 per cent in 1991, and foreign trade turnover among the six countries also diminished to a fraction of its previous level.[2] As a consequence of this, a massive share of East European industrial enterprises immediately went bankrupt.

According to some Western economists, East European statistics

---

2 *Business Eastern Europe*, The Economist Intelligence Unit, 21 October 1991.

are misleading about the countries' economic performance, since those statistics do not encompass the results of myriads of the newly created small private businesses: had the economic achievements of those small businesses been taken into account, the economic decline would not be as steep as is reflected in the official statistics.[3] There is some truth in this argument. In particular, private retail trading, catering, real estate markets and other personal services are booming in the East European countries, and this is not sufficiently accounted for in the statistics. However, the fact that a considerable share of private companies do nothing but 'suck away' the assets of state-owned enterprises or carry out black market export–import and currency operations (or both), is covered by a thick fog. (The reason for doing business illegally, in Hungary or Poland, for instance, is not that economic regulation is not liberal enough for such private activities: the 'rationale' behind these activities is usually pure tax evasion and, in addition, exploitation of monopoly positions.) Thus, the other extreme interpretation, namely that there exists a robust private economy in the East European countries whose performance is just not reported properly by the statistical offices, should be avoided as well.

The most glaring sign of the structural deficiencies and economic imbalances was a high and accelerating rate of inflation in each East European country. The year 1992 brought a turnaround in the Czech and Slovak Federal Republic and in Hungary. The former country reported a zero rate of inflation for the first five months of 1992.[4] By the end of the year, the inflation rate was expected to remain below 7 per cent. In Hungary, the rate of inflation diminished to a 'mere' 22 per cent during the first six months on an annual basis; consumer price inflation was not expected to exceed 25 per cent for the whole year either, and as regards producers' prices their increase was predicted to be less than 12 per cent for 1992. In the Russian Federation inflation is still skyrocketing and it is on the rise in Poland as well.

Among the factors that contribute to the rising inflation, we can

3 See, for example, Sachs (1990), pp.19–24.
4 This figure is somewhat suspicious, because it may not include so-called 'new products and services' whose prices are much higher than the traditional comparable products and services.

identify conventional and also genuinely 'socialist' ones. The most consequential conventional factor is a persistent deficit of the state budget that has been present in almost each country since the mid-1980s. In some cases, such as Poland and the former USSR, the size of the deficit itself was large enough to result in extreme financial strain. At the same time, it was true for all countries that the structure of the deficit and that of government expenditures lay at the heart of the problem. Most notably, huge production subsidies together with subsidies on consumption turned into illusions any attempt by the central authorities to constrain reckless spending by enterprises and governments. By the same token, easy access to state subsidies encouraged enterprises to raise prices without restraint.

Another important factor in domestic inflation has been a substantial export surplus needed by some East European countries in order to finance their external debt. This phenomenon was not specific for Eastern Europe: it was extensively known in most developing countries as well.[5]

The most decisive and really genuine factors of the East European inflation were the following:

(1) a massive and successive increase in wages that bore no relation to labour productivity or the profitability of enterprises; and

(2) a 'snowball'-type indebtedness of the enterprises to one another. Thus, enterprises stopped paying for deliveries, by this action forcing the sellers to do the same with their own suppliers. The total amount of so-called 'enterprise queuing' added up to 10–12 per cent of the annual GDP in Hungary in 1990–91.[6] In 1992, the amount of forced, inter-enterprise credits increased even further and it reached 15 per cent of the GDP. The magnitude of enterprise liabilities was similar in Poland and the ČSFR, and it was even higher in Russia and the other member states of the Commonwealth of Independent States (CIS).

There is a consensus among economists that the economic crisis of the East European countries cannot be resolved without restoring financial balance and controlling inflation. However, the nature of the inflationary pressures in a command economy or in an economy in transition caution us that no quick stabilization is feasible if financial stability is desired. In particular, the last two factors discussed above,

5   See, for example, Sachs (1989).
6   I have discussed this issue in detail in Major (1991d).

namely wage increases and 'enterprise queuing', require a firm approach. In principle, the rate of inflation can be slashed within a very short period of time, but financial stability cannot be maintained for long without deep structural and institutional changes in the post-communist economies. Institutional changes must mean, first of all, a comprehensive liberalization of the economic regulations and an unambiguous disentanglement of the state bureaucracy and economic organizations. In addition, and in close connection with these requirements, radical changes must include the formation of transparent and sensible institutions to uphold private property rights. But how far and how fast can and should privatization of the state-owned property proceed? Why is privatization an adequate answer to the economic crisis of the East European countries? These are the issues we shall turn to next.

4. The Reasons for Privatization

It is a common conviction in Eastern Europe, widely shared by economists and the public at large, that the long-term poor performance and the final collapse of the command economies can ultimately be traced back to the overwhelming 'state' or 'collective' ownership of properties. Privatization of the majority of state-owned property is considered by most people to be a necessary precondition for a sound economy to develop. However, the international economic literature is far from unanimous on this point. Several economists argue that it is not the form of ownership but the type of organization and management of companies that determines economic efficiency and performance. (The best-known representative of this school is John Kenneth Galbraith.) This school has tried to show that state-owned enterprises can be as efficient as private ones if they operate in a competitive market environment and their managers are selected in competition, on their professional merits. Kornai, himself an unambiguous advocate of dominant private ownership, also emphasized that his reasoning for privatization is based on the values of liberalism which he shares, and the reasons for privatization cannot be derived from purely positive economic theory.[1]

In principle, the above arguments in favour of a 'neutral' approach to state or private ownership might be true, but in practice, it is extremely difficult to find facts that would support them. The long-term experience of countries in East and West shows that state or public ownership of companies is organically connected to the exclusion of market competition, to monopolistic tendencies of companies and to over-bureaucratization of company management. Managers of the state-owned companies are usually selected by

---

1 Kornai (1990), pp.21–2.

politicians who want managers to boost political goals rather than productive efficiency.[2]

At the same time, there may be factors present in some sectors of the economy where public ownership with limited competition is a more efficient way of organizing economic activities than unconstrained markets. The classical cases are 'natural' monopolies (such as, for example, railways, electricity networks) and economic sectors where externalities prevail (such as environmental protection or defence). Evidence shows, however, that the boundaries between the competitive sectors and the natural monopolies or sectors with externalities are not set once and for all. Those boundaries may change when deregulation and market competition become feasible and more efficient forms than public monopolies. The boundaries usually tighten on natural monopolies, as in the case of telecommunications, for instance. Apart from the sectors mentioned above, there is no real reason to accept that state ownership can be superior or equal to private ownership as regards economic efficiency. In fact, all the evidence shows that a dominant 'state' ownership – or as we called it, '*nomenklatura*' ownership – has been the most decisive basic institution of the command economies that determined their economic performance and guided those economies towards irreversible decay.

A final aspect of state *versus* private ownership must be emphasized as regards Eastern Europe. At a first glance, there might be substantial similarities between state ownership in developed market economies and in command economies. For instance, Kornai went so far as to say that the differences are of a quantitative rather than qualitative nature.[3] However, this observation is misguided. As Lindbeck (1973) correctly pointed out, the role and forms of state involvement in market economies with dominant private ownership are completely different from the role of the communist state in the economy. I also have argued that the communist states had almost unconstrained authority over the economy, administering a complex system of overall political regulation that differed qualitatively ('by nature') from well-defined public ownership within market economies.[4] Consequently, while the historical experience of private

2 See, for example, Montemartini (1967) and Wicksell (1967).
3 Kornai (1986), pp.1699-1700.
4 Major (1991b), pp.10-16.

ownership and privatization in the West might be relevant to the East European countries in transition, the existence of public ownership in developed market economies is not an argument in favour of retaining state ownership in Eastern Europe.

In the next two sections I shall briefly list the main reasons for the privatization of state-owned property in Eastern Europe, as those reasons were presented by economists and politicians in the West and in the East. However, first it is necessary to define, or at least clarify, what privatization is. I use the term 'privatization' for the full conversion of property rights from the state or collective owners to private owners. After privatization, the property rights of private owners cannot be constrained in any other way than by the constitution or by acts of parliament in order to defend the basic rights of a country's population and comply with basic international laws. It is in accord with the above definition that the state can retain the property rights of public goods, provided that public goods are defined by democratically elected political institutions. However, I do not consider as privatization the conversion of state-owned enterprises into limited liability companies or joint stock companies where the shareholders are other state-owned enterprises or commercial banks. Consequently, so-called 'spontaneous' or 'wild' privatizations cannot be regarded as real privatizations. (This issue is discussed in detail below.) A clear distinction must be made between privatization and commercialization, or any other way of replacing the old forms of 'collective' ownership with new ones. (The latter case is called *razgosudarstvlenie* – 'destatization' – in the Soviet literature.[5]) Moreover, I do not regard a company as having been privatized if the majority share of its property is still owned by the state, or the state has a dominant voting right among the company's owners.

---

5 On the confusion about defining property rights in the former USSR see, for example, Hanson (1990) and Filatotchev, Buck and Wright (1992). Hanson's arguments are well supported by a former law on 'commercialization' and 'privatization' signed by Gorbachev in July 1991: see *Izvestiya*, 8 August 1991.

4.1 REASONS FOR PRIVATIZATION IN THE WESTERN LITERATURE

This section can be very concise, since most of the economic and some of the political reasons for privatization have been marshalled by other authors: therefore, it is sufficient just to mention them briefly. Von Mises (1935) and von Hayek (1944) strongly argued against state ownership on the basis that state ownership and central planning of an economy are not viable. North (North and Thomas, 1973, and North, 1981) drew the general conclusion, based on a detailed historical analysis, that an economy's productive and allocative efficiencies are ultimately determined by its institution of property rights. Whenever the property rights are unclear, this always results in a considerable deterioration of economic efficiency. North further argued that private property rights provide the most transparent and efficient framework for a complex set of economic activities. Alchian and Demsetz (1973), then Furubotn and Pejovich (1974), reasoned along similar lines.

Kornai (1990), Grosfeld (1990), Lipton and Sachs (1990), Åslund (1991a, 1991b) and Blanchard *et al.* (1991) also placed economic efficiency in the centre of discussion. They all argued that only responsible private owners can be expected to utilize resources efficiently, while public or state ownership usually results in careless spending by the company managers, in wasteful resource allocation and in a lack of the company's flexibility. In addition, Åslund and also Pelikan[6] stressed that 'creative destruction' (in a Schumpeterian sense) and perpetual innovation can be expected only from private entrepreneurs. Kornai emphasized that a hard budget constraint can exist only for privately-owned companies, but not for enterprises financed or supported by the state budget. Sachs pointed out that the most imminent danger East European countries face is a tearaway hyperinflation and the ensuing financial collapse of the countries concerned. He traced the unrestrained wage claims of employees of the state-owned enterprises as a major factor in the inflationary pressure. According to Sachs, the only effective constraint on sky-rocketing wages in the longer run can be private ownership.

6 Pelikan (1990).

As regards the political aspects of privatization, Milton Friedman, Grosfeld, Åslund and Lipton and Sachs emphasized that political democracy is only emerging in Eastern Europe. Without a sound market economy and extensive private ownership the danger of a backlash in the democratization process is always present. Thus, privatization is the best way to create the solid foundations of a viable democracy.[7] Beside these authors, Blanchard *et al.* also warned that without swift and comprehensive privatization initiated by the state, a peculiar form of 'wild' or 'spontaneous' privatization, namely expropriation of the national assets by members of the communist *nomenklatura*, might come, or indeed it was already happening. In fact, Friedman, Blanchard *et al.* and Lipton and Sachs considered this danger to be the most important reason for, and a driving force of, privatization in Eastern Europe. It may certainly be true that 'wild privatization' of state-owned property by managers of the military-industrial complex and by members of the KGB was a real danger in the former USSR. There is some evidence to support the assumption that managers of the state-owned enterprises, the KGB and the mafia worked closely together, and the bulk of the state-owned property might have ended up in the hands of those groups. Similar dangers are present in Bulgaria and Romania as well.

So-called '*nomenklatura* companies' were also established in large numbers in Poland. However, a substantial part of those companies remained in state hands: that is, they were not privatized by the old *nomenklatura*. What really irritated Polish people was that managers of the state-owned enterprises set up their own private companies from their own resources, but they exploited the extensive shortages. In particular, private companies provided customers with goods that were not available from the state-owned enterprises directed by the very same managers who owned the private companies. In Hungary, attacks on 'spontaneous privatizations' by the old *nomenklatura* were based less on facts than on political aims of different pressure groups. The issue was almost wholly irrelevant in the former GDR. Several Western authors based their arguments on privatization on scattered

---

7 However, as Comisso (1991) pointed out very convincingly, political democracy, that is, the 'rule of majority', cannot always be reconciled with liberalism, especially with a liberal economic policy.

anecdotal evidence rather than on hard facts when they stressed the issue of spontaneous privatization.

While tremendous emphasis was devoted by Western scholars – and by some East European politicians – to the abuses of privatization by the old *nomenklatura*, these authors failed to mention the most crucial aspect of privatization that may easily determine the whole process for decades and its final outcome. This is that privatization is extremely important in Eastern Europe since it is the only way of breaking up the massive system of political regulation of the economy. Without the birth of autonomous private owners, the entanglement of the political state and of the economic bureaucracy and management will prevail, and a command economy, built on ideological foundations other than communism this time, will re-emerge. Kornai, Grosfeld and Åslund put the disentanglement of politics and the economy on their list of reasons for privatization, but they also considered 'spontaneous privatization' the most important issue to tackle.

Building the strategy of privatization on the assumption that the most important issue to be sorted out is preventing former managers and government bureaucrats from benefiting from their position can very easily lead to the derailment of the whole process. It is easy to reach the conclusion that what is needed is to replace members of the old *nomenklatura* by new 'democratic' managers, and the rest will come automatically. This approach is popular among the newly elected governments in Eastern Europe, too. But the real danger for political democracy and for an emerging market economy with private ownership is precisely the victory of this 'solution'. Removing heads, and replacing them with newly emerging ones, would serve as a substitute for profound institutional changes, while a politically regulated economy would survive and it could become the basis of a new dictatorship or totalitarian regime. At the same time, it is the new political elites rather than former managers who are to blame if the new elites promote members of the old *nomenklatura* to high positions in the state-owned enterprises whose privatization is planned. In that way, old managers who want to save their skins are turned into loyal supporters of the new elites, but this is completely different from 'wild privatization'. It must be the constitution and the laws that set the rules, and it must not be the new governments or political parties that select who will suit them best as private owners. Criminal practices of the old (and new) *nomenklatura* must face legal charges on an individual basis, but a group of people cannot be stigmatized as *ab ovo* criminals.[8] Thus, spontaneous privatization must get proportional and adequate attention in the privatization debate – presumably much less than is reflected in the mainstream Western literature on the subject.

However obvious it may sound, it is not easy to accept that capitalism cannot develop without capitalists,[9] and company managers are suitable candidates for the job since they have the accumulated knowledge of how to exercise property rights effectively. It must be the law and a sensitive economic policy that prevents managers from exploiting the acquired property for their own benefit alone, rather than a politically motivated campaign against the managers of the state-owned enterprises.

4.2   ADDITIONAL REASONS FOR PRIVATIZATION IN THE EAST

Most of the reasons for privatization listed above are widely shared, at least in principle, by East European economists and governments. But the list is not exhaustive. During the last two or three years, several other arguments for privatization have emerged in Eastern Europe. In fact, the 'East European reasons' have become even more important guiding forces in the privatization debate than the rationalized economic arguments raised by Western economists. Most of the arguments for privatization marshalled in Eastern Europe have been based on traditionalist and emotional considerations rather than on current economic analysis.

According to influential political groups and parties, the first and most decisive reason for privatization is 'to do justice' to those who had owned properties before the communist takeovers in Eastern Europe, and whose properties were confiscated by the communist regimes. The advocates of a full or partial reprivatization of

8 The birth of a new *nomenklatura* is extensively discussed in Bujak (1991), especially p.153.
9 Winiecki (1990) correctly emphasized this point.

state-owned properties argue that the 'sanctity of private ownership' cannot be restored in Eastern Europe until all confiscated properties are returned to the original owners. Inviting claims for nationalized or confiscated properties began privatization in Eastern Germany after reunification, and reprivatization also became the focus of discussion in Czechoslovakia, Poland and in Hungary.[10] (In Germany, about 1.5 million property claims were submitted to the *Treuhandanstalt*; in other countries, the interest of former owners in recovering their properties was more lukewarm than in Germany.)

Since the issue of reprivatization was put on the agenda and the actual reprivatization process started in Eastern Europe, it created confusion and controversy to such an extent that it could not enhance the security of private property rights. As a matter of principle, reprivatization can result in at least as much injustice to some as the justice it provides to one particular group of the population. In practice, actually administering the collection and approval of claims, then distributing properties or vouchers of compensation for the confiscated properties, has proved to be an unfeasible task for the government bureaucracy to tackle even in Germany, let alone in other East European countries. At the same time, the reprivatization debate and the ensuing administrative process of restitution blocked or retarded other forms of privatization in the East European countries. Reprivatization claims made foreign investors especially feel insecure, since each reprivatization case may involve a series of legal suits.

A special case of reprivatization is the restitution of different churches that lost their properties after the Second World War. Freedom of religion was one of the basic human rights the peoples of Eastern Europe have been deprived of for decades. Consequently, restoration of religious liberty is an important component of restoring individual freedom in these countries, without which - among other factors - free enterprise and a liberal market economy can hardly develop. To fulfil their role, existing churches need material assets (real estate, budgetary resources, etc.) also. On these grounds, the churches' claims for properties and financial resources, and the East European governments' endeavour to provide them, are reasonable and widely accepted by political parties and social groups in Eastern

10 For Hungary, see, for example, *RFE Report on Eastern Europe*, 10 May 1991, pp.7-11.

Europe. The zeal of religious leaders and East European governments turns into an unacceptable striving at the point when these groups, with the support of populist and 'historical conservative' political parties, refer to the religious and political role of the churches – mainly the Catholic or the Orthodox church – before and during the Second World War, as a legitimate and legal basis for their current claims for property. In this scenario, reprivatization of religious properties does not serve the cause of privatization in Eastern Europe, but rather represents a retreat to the political and economic conditions of the pre-war era. At the same time, restitution of ownership to individuals and churches occupies the centre of attention, diverting interest and energies from other, at least equally important, aspects of the transformation of property rights.

A third element of the politically and historically motivated approaches to privatization in Eastern Europe is the search for and creation of a middle class by some political parties. These political groups envisage future capitalism in Eastern Europe as a bipolar political and economic system built on millions of small private entrepreneurs on the one hand, and a strong central state on the other. The historical roots of this vision reach back to the Weimar Republic in Germany in the 1920s, and the Gömbös–Imrédy regime in Hungary in the late 1930s. In such a system, small entrepreneurs and petty bourgeoisie are autonomous economic agents but they are in no position to control or limit the political or economic power of the state. The groups of small private owners are created by a selective process – administered or guided by the state – to help loyal groups to acquire properties.[11] The catchwords of this approach are gratitude, loyalty and dependence that bind the newly created owners to the governing political forces. In this respect, the idea of 'capitalism with small entrepreneurs' and the concept of restitution are not far from each other.[12]

Finally, there exists a complex group of arguments for privatization that are connected to the current financial problems of the East

11 Some of the issues discussed above had been touched upon by Stark (1990) in the case of Hungary.
12 The title of Åslund's article in *Dagens Nyheter* (a leading Swedish daily), 27 October 1991, was revealing: it read, 'Ryssland ny naziststat' ('Russia, a new nazi state'). That is, the phenomena that accompany an emerging dictatorship, familiar in some Central European countries, are not unknown in the former Soviet republics either.

European states rather than to past historical regimes. Privatization is considered by influential groups of the East European governments and by the ministerial bureaucracy as a means of restoring the financial balance of these countries. Financial imbalances have several facets in Eastern Europe. In part, communist states accumulated a huge internal government debt over the past forty years, by launching numerous gigantic and prestigious development projects that mostly yielded losses. In addition, government debt increased automatically because East European governments could 'borrow' money from their national bank *de facto* free of charge, without paying interest. Especially in countries such as Hungary and Poland, where inflation accelerated considerably during the last decade, the difference between the market rate of interest and the very low interest rate paid by the government automatically added to the government's debt.

The deficit of the state budget – a non-negligible share of the government's debt – constituted the most immediate pressure on the East European governments to find additional resources for their budget expenditures. They considered the revenue that could be acquired from selling state-owned property as a good prospect to meet their financial needs. The danger of using revenues from the sale of properties in order to fill the gaps in the state budget was loudly voiced by economists. Since such a government practice would mean a conversion of state-owned assets into money flows, the revenues from the sales would have been irresponsibly wasted by central bureaucracies. However, the East European governments' temptation to 'grab' an easy source of income and use this income to recover their fading popularity was too great.

Another aspect of this approach is connected to the severe external debt in convertible currencies of most East European countries. Governments regarded a part of the state-owned assets as goods to be sold to foreign investors, and wanted to use the hard currency revenues to reduce the country's debt. In addition, they also hoped that foreign direct investment would bring new technology and management skills into the ailing East European industries. During the past four years, each country has passed a law on foreign direct investment to facilitate acquisitions by foreigners. However, both the popular and official attitudes towards foreign acquisition differed considerably across countries. For instance, in Poland the parliament introduced severe restrictions on foreign acquisitions in the 1990 Act on Privatization.[13] In Czechoslovakia, where the privatization debate was in its preliminary phase compared with Poland in early 1991, voices were also raised against 'selling off the country' to foreigners. The Hungarian regulation has been very liberal towards foreign investors, but in actual cases controversies about 'too large a role of foreigners' in the Hungarian economy surfaced successively.[14] In reality, foreign acquisition of East European state-owned properties has been the main form of privatization so far, as will be discussed in detail in the next chapter.

The different reasons and ideologies for privatization outlined above are not exclusive; rather, they complement each other in the current East European debates on privatization. Consequently, it is not a single trend but an amalgam of different approaches that shapes the East European governments' plans for privatization. What is decisive for those plans are the relative weights of the often controversial endeavours of competing political groups inside and outside the governments.

13 'Act on the Privatization ...' op.cit.; see also Michalski (1991), p.329. In June 1991 some relaxation of the restrictions occurred after the Agency of Foreign Investments had been dissolved: see *Gazeta Bankowa*, No.45, 10–16 November 1991.
14 *Euromoney*, March 1991, pp.41–8; and *Financial Times*, 14 May 1991.

5. Plans and Realities of Privatization in Eastern Europe

East European countries began the theoretical debates and the elaboration of programmes for privatization in different years. In Hungary, a programme of 'pseudo-privatization' was set out by Tibor Liska as early as 1972.[1] Liska's main idea was to distribute state-owned property as a 'heritage of the society as a whole' free of charge among all citizens. Then a nationwide auctioning off of the distributed properties should have started among 'pseudo-owners'. (I call the owners created by Liska's method 'pseudo-owners', because Liska wanted to impose a rule of compulsory sale of properties by the owners in cases where anyone came forward with a more lucrative promise regarding profits than the rate of profit earned by the incumbent owners.) Another early proposal for transforming the prevailing state ownership into a form of 'institutional ownership' (mainly property rights allocated to holding companies) was published by Márton Tardos in 1972.[2] However, the first real breakthrough in Hungary came as late as 1988–89, when the legal acts on economic associations, foreign investment and enterprise transformation were passed by the Hungarian parliament.[3] Since then, several legal regulations have been adopted by the parliament both before and after the free national elections.[4]

Apart from Hungary, Poland went the furthest in developing various plans for privatization. Other East European countries began to 'define' the issues of privatization only at the end of the 1980s and early 1990s. Privatization, particularly the implementation of the

---

1 Liska (1985).
2 Tardos (1972).
3 Act VI/1988 (X.10.), *Magyar Közlöny*, No.47 (1988), Act XXIV/1988 (XII.12.), *Magyar Közlöny*, No.69 (1988) and Act XIII/1989 (VI.13.), *Magyar Közlöny*, No.38 (1989).
4 I discussed the successive laws affecting privatization in Major (1991a,b).

'voucher scheme', began to accelerate in the ČSFR only in mid-1992. A comprehensive privatization programme surfaced in Russia and in some other CIS countries also in 1992. Privatization coupons worth R10,000 were soon to be distributed among the population of Russia, and other CIS states also regard free distribution as a main road towards dominant private ownership in their countries. Other forms, such as sale to foreigners and to managers and workers at a discounted price, are also envisaged in these various countries.[5]

5.1 THE INITIAL FRAMEWORK OF THE GOVERNMENTS' PLANS FOR PRIVATIZATION

In the CSFR, discussions about privatization started in 1989 and a proposal for the so-called 'voucher scheme' has been on the agenda since the very beginning of the privatization process. Other ideas received much less attention.[6] Serious proposals for privatization were published by academics in Poland, also in 1988–89. The most articulate of these were elaborated by Stefan Kawalec, Janusz Lewandowski and Jan Szomburg and in the volume edited by Janusz Beksiak and Jan Winiecki.[7] Plans for privatization emerged only after the radical political changes in the ČSFR, Bulgaria and Romania, and along with the creation of a monetary and political union of the two Germanies in the former GDR. In the Soviet republics ideas of privatization started to overshadow 'de-étatization' or commercialization (*razgosudarstvlenie*) of state-owned enterprises only after the failed coup in August 1991. In 1992, after the disintegration of the former USSR, the governments of the Baltic republics, followed by the Russian government, outlined their privatization programmes that focused on the free distribution of state-owned properties, and on the property acquisition of the employees of the state-owned enterprises. Moreover, in the Baltic republics, an extensive restoration of

5 See, for example, Frydman *et al.* (1993a,b).
6 See, for example, Klacek *et al.* (1992), Kluson (1992), and Janacková and Janáček (1992).
7 Kawalec (1989), Lewandowski and Szomburg (1989), Beksiak and Winiecki (eds) (1990).

confiscated property to its original owners was also proposed by the governments.

There is no single blueprint of privatization by the governments of any of the East European countries that could be used as an authentic basis of reference to compare plans and actual results. It is perhaps in the ČSFR that the government's plan is fairly unambiguous and straightforward. However, during the autumn of 1991, the Klaus-Triska plan for privatization (the so-called 'voucher scheme') also came under fierce attack in the federal parliament.[8] In November of that year, the implementation of the voucher scheme was suspended and postponed for three months.[9] The Polish law of July 1990 on privatization became obsolete by late 1991, since a new plan for the free distribution of a substantial share of state-owned assets had been put forward by the government. However, parliament did not endorse this plan until mid-1992, and it remains to be seen what will happen to the privatization plans of the former Bielecki government after a second 'shock therapy' - this time political in nature - that was conducted by the Polish electorate in the national elections of 27 October 1991.[10] Following several abortive attempts to form a viable government, the new Polish government and Prime Minister Mme Suchocka seem more likely to succeed in overcoming the chaos that had emerged after the elections.

In Hungary, the new government's successive 'Programmes for National Revival', then a programme compiled by the new Finance Minister Mihály Kupa in February 1991, and the 'Guidelines for Management Policy of the National Assets for 1991' that were submitted to parliament in September 1991, all reflect a pragmatic approach to privatization. Specifically, in each document it was clearly stated that the Hungarian government's intention was to privatize 40-50 per cent of the state-owned assets by the end of 1994. Moreover, all documents revealed the government's intention to separate legal acts on different aspects of privatization that had been

8 See, for example, Martin (1991a).

9 *Business Eastern Europe, Business International*, 25 November 1991, pp.421-2.

10 As is well known, no political party managed to win a decisive share of the parliamentary seats in the latest Polish elections (1991). The party that came out of the elections the strongest was the Democratic Union (led by former Prime Minister Mazowiecki), and the pseudo-communist Peasants' Party was the fourth strongest political formation: see *Rzeczpospolita*, 31 October 1991. Together these parties may have a majority in parliament.

endorsed by either the former or the newly elected parliament. However, a comprehensive programme or law on privatization still does not exist in Hungary.

Until June 1992, government control and administration of all privatization was concentrated in the State Property Agency in Hungary. But then parliament adopted the laws on 'Permanent State Ownership' and on 'Temporary State Ownership'. The first Act created a new government organization, the so-called 'State Holding Company Ltd' (SHC). The SHC was entitled to exercise all property rights of the state over those assets that the government wanted to retain in state ownership for a longer period. Thus, a bipolar government control of privatization and property rights emerged. The 'connecting link' between the two bodies is the newly appointed Minister for Privatization, who supervises both organizations.[11]

In Eastern Germany, the German government's privatization programme was built on two pillars: first, the restitution of those state-owned properties whose former owners came forward with their claims; and secondly the restructuring and selling off of state-owned enterprises by a newly created privatization agency, the *Treuhandanstalt*, to bidders making the most favourable offer.[12]

In Romania, a law on privatization was passed by parliament in August 1991.[13] This law, together with legal regulations on foreign investment, constitutes the framework of privatization in that country. However, the emphasis is put by the Romanian government very much on attracting foreign investors rather than offering a comprehensive programme of privatization. Privatization programmes also surfaced in Albania,[14] Bulgaria[15] and the republics of a disintegrating USSR.[16]

In addition to the official documents of privatization – documents that have been elaborated by different, and frequently competing, government agencies – several comprehensive or piecemeal proposals for privatization were written by outside advisers, academics, formal

11 See, for example, *Figyelő*, 2 July 1992.
12 See, for example, Schrettl (1992).
13 *Financial Times*, 17 October 1991.
14 See Åslund and Sjöberg (1991).
15 See *Östekonomisk Rapport*, Vol.3, No.8, 21 October 1991.
16 *Sovetskaya Rossiya*, No.205, 29 October 1991, and Frydman *et al.* (1993b).

and informal gatherings of the representatives of different political parties and leaders of social organizations, such as the trade unions. As regards the number of participants, the 'privatization game' was the most colourful and complex in Hungary, Poland and in the former USSR (chiefly in Russia and the Baltic republics). Proposals or even *ad hoc* ideas for privatization could influence the government's thinking to a considerable extent provided those ideas were in line with the political endeavours of influential government officials. Alternatively, these proposals could have an impact on the official privatization policy if they were backed by forces substantial enough to 'convince' the government. Such proposals included, for instance, the recommendation to the government of an employees' stock-ownership plan (ESOP), special rules covering a loan disbursement plan to support the acquisition of assets by private purchasers, and case-by-case 'manual control' of individual privatization deals by the government in order to favour predetermined social groups with substantial political influence. I shall mention such proposals occasionally when they appear to be relevant to a government's privatization programme, although my principal focus will be on the official plans of privatization. Now, rather than reviewing the different privatization programmes of the various European governments one by one, I shall first discuss the main aspects and directions of the plans, and then I shall present the evidence of the actual accomplishments in privatization to date in the various countries.

5.2 PLANS FOR PRIVATIZATION

The main issues of the plans for privatization of the East European governments can be listed as follows:

(1) How should privatization be defined? Specifically, what is the relationship between privatization and 'ownership reform' or 'de-étatization', or even commercialization of state-owned assets and enterprises?

(2) How large a share of the state-owned property must be privatized? In addition, what part of the industrial and infrastructural assets can be privatized without limitation, and which are the sectors or economic activities where state ownership should be retained? This

issue is closely connected to the envisaged role of foreign investors in the privatization process.

(3) What are the qualitatively different groups of state-owned property that require different methods of privatization? And a prior question: how can sensible criteria be determined at all, by which those groups can be distinguished?

(4) How rapidly should privatization proceed? Does speed depend on the type of properties?

And finally,

(5) What institutions and methods can and should be used in privatization? This is the issue that relates most directly to the question of who the winners and the losers of privatization will be, and to the problem of sufficient demand for properties. As regards the methods of privatization, the participation of foreign investors must be mentioned here again. Property acquisition by foreigners is considered to be the 'mainstream' of privatization by most East European governments. However, the governments' striving to attract foreign investors can and does contradict their endeavours to mollify domestic opposition to acquisitions by foreigners (see (2) above).

5.2.1 What is Privatization?

A clear definition of or framework for privatization[17] and clear criteria for identifying when a piece of property or an enterprise can be considered as having been privatized are absent in the thinking behind the privatization programmes of the East European governments. The Western literature on privatization is immense, but the traditional ideas and methods of privatization are mostly inapplicable to the East European efforts to convert state-owned property into private property.[18] Hodjera proposed a definition that attached great impor-

---

17 It is frequently emphasized by economists that privatization is not an exact concept in economics, but a 'code name' for a very complex process that is more political than economic. It is true that political considerations influence privatization in developed market economies, too. However, a major accomplishment of Western political economy was to incorporate political interests into the 'economic game': see, for example, Brennan and Buchanan (1985), and Vickers and Yarrow (1988), especially Chapters 2–4.

18 To mention but a few theoretical studies on Western privatization: Bishop and Kay (1988), Jones (1990), Sappington (1987), Shapiro and Willig (1990), and Vogelsang (1990).

tance to a full transfer of property rights from public to private owners (in most cases, physical persons), and to majority share-owning and voting rights for those private owners.[19] He emphasized that a public company with minority private shareholders cannot be considered privatized. On the other hand, public (state) institutions can have a minority stake in a private company and that company can still be regarded as privately owned. However, the above approach – or, as a matter of fact, any clear-cut definition of privatization – is not fully accepted by the East European governments. Governments' progress reports on privatization often compound the share of private capital invested in the economy with the share of privately-owned companies or assets. Moreover, privatization and commercialization of state-owned enterprises are confused as well. This confusion is best reflected in the debates and popular attacks on 'wild privatization' or 'spontaneous privatization' of state-owned enterprises by the communist *nomenklatura*. Unfortunately, knowledgeable Western economists, such as David Lipton and Jeffrey Sachs, or Olivier Blanchard and Richard Layard, have not avoided this trap of confusion either.[20]

As has been extensively discussed in the literature, before the political revolutions in Eastern Europe, but after the adoption of the legal acts on enterprise transformation by the late communist parliaments in Hungary and Poland, managers of the state-owned enterprises started converting their companies into closed joint stock companies or a group of limited liability companies.[21] However, managers retained the most important rights of managerial decision making through a holding company that was set up by them as an umbrella organization standing over the limited liability companies. The main driving force behind the enterprise transformations was the avoidance of the company's bankruptcy and liquidation, and even though legal grounds were created for an enterprise's conversion, enterprise managers did not act on their own: in most cases they were encouraged by the government. In the same manner, they were supported by the central bureaucracy in the search for foreign

19 Hodjera (1991), pp.274–5.
20 See Lipton and Sachs (1990) and Blanchard *et al.* (1991). A summary of some Western proposals for East European privatization is given by Borensztein and Kumar (1991).
21 See, for example, Grosfeld (1990), Dąbrowski (1991), and Voszka (1991a,b,c).

investors in their companies. For instance, in Hungary in 1989, even ministers made up long lists of state-owned companies that were considered suitable for sale to foreigners. Ministries even 'forgot' to notify the managers of the enterprises beforehand, then several ministers travelled to the West in an attempt to use those lists to attract foreign buyers.

The situation before the political changes took place can best be described as a final phase in the previous trends of confusion over property rights that ended in complete chaos, rather than the managers' deliberate attempt to 'steal' state property. What enterprise managers did was try to exercise the *de facto* property rights that had been granted to enterprises by the central leadership since the mid-1980s. However, managers could not actually *de jure* sell state-owned property either to themselves or to outside buyers (such cases also did occur, or were attempted, on rare occasions, but these deals were illegal according to the prevailing law); enterprise assets that had been converted into limited liability or joint stock companies still remained in state hands.

The real problem surfaces now when genuine private owners take over parts of an enterprise or, more importantly, sections of an enterprise's shareholders. Let us assume, for instance, that a state-owned commercial bank has a share of 40 per cent in a state-owned company. As a next step, 70 per cent of the commercial bank's assets is sold to private investors. Will that mean that 40 per cent of the enterprise's ownership rights has automatically passed into private hands? Or will the enterprise in question be privatized by this action to the extent of 28 per cent? This issue is critical for the enterprise and for the bank as well, since 40 per cent of ownership is usually large enough to secure a controlling position, whereas 28 per cent might not be. These and other problems cannot be sorted out without a comprehensive legal and institutional framework of privatization, and that framework cannot work in practice if basic definitions are not designed in the most transparent and rational way possible.

It seems to me that a reasonable way to proceed is to make a sharp distinction among de-étatization, commercialization and privatization of state-owned assets and enterprises. De-étatization would consist in the transfer of property rights to anyone or any community other than the institutions and organizations of the central state. In other words, transferring property rights of certain assets from the central state to municipal governments, or working collectives, as well as selling or distributing state-owned property to genuine private owners, could be considered de-étatization. Commercialization of an enterprise means the full economic autonomy of its staff – including the transformation of the enterprise into different forms – except the right to sell the enterprise's assets (or, more generally, excluding the sale of the enterprise's property rights). Finally, privatization means the full transfer of the property rights from non-private to genuinely private owners. (This definition allows for the state or local government to hold a minority stake in a company's assets, as described by Hodjera, but only at the discretion of the private owners.)

Next, general rules must be defined that impose limitations on private owners in exercising their property rights. These constraints must be included in the Constitution and they must be approved by the broadest democratic consensus. A few further, but normative – that is, non-discretionary and non-negotiable – restrictions can affect specific economic sectors or economic activities where public utilities and public goods prevail. Apart from these general rules, the guiding principle must be that everything is within the power of private owners that is not prohibited by the legal constraints mentioned above.

A specific but more and more decisive issue in East European privatizations is the role of reprivatization or restitution of the properties that had been nationalized by the communist regimes. Formally speaking, restitution is a genuine way of privatizing state property, a method, moreover, that meets the criteria of privatization mentioned above. However, the legal basis of claims for confiscated properties can be controversial, notably in those cases when recovering properties by the original owners would violate the property rights of others. From a 'constitutional' point of view, reprivatization should be limited to those cases when restitution would not infringe other persons' property rights, and it should be accomplished in such a manner as to avoid that. From the point of view of the economy, restitution should be completely avoided, since it diverts the attention and energies of the peoples of Eastern Europe from the most crucial issues of economic transformation and from the feasible ways of achieving transformation with the least possible amount of pain and sacrifices.

Finally, it should be mentioned that private ownership is not developing in Eastern Europe exclusively via privatization, since thousands of new, private businesses and companies are being created in each country every year. However, important as this trend is in the transformation process, it is beyond the scope of this study.

5.2.2 The Desirable Size of the Private Sector and its Composition

There is no defined limit in the plans of the East European governments as to how far privatization should go. What is usually specified is the governments' intention to reduce the share of state ownership from the currently prevailing 85-90 per cent to about 50 per cent within 3-4 years. However, the composition of the other half of the assets is vaguely defined, and it usually includes different types of non-state ownership, such as properties allocated to the local governments and other forms of institutional ownership (for example, insurance and pension funds).

It would be unrealistic to expect a precise figure to be set by a government for the private sector's share in the distant future. It could even be harmful if privatization became the subject of central planning, and consequently of 'plan bargaining'. But it is equally detrimental to privatization if governments are reluctant to give up their ownership rights, or are willing to do so in a controversial process that drags on for several years.

Recently, a number of mathematical models have been developed to prove the assumption that a 'critical mass' of privatization is the most decisive factor in ensuring a high probability of success, or at least the irreversibility of the privatization process.[22] These authors showed that a privatization campaign cannot be successful – or it may not become irreversible – unless the amount of the privatized property passes a certain threshold. In a model built on fairly simple assumptions, this threshold is 50 per cent of all properties. A critical mass of privatization implies not only the scope but also the speed by

22 See, for example, Roland and Verdier (1991), and Laban and Wolf (1991).

which privatization must progress if it is to be irreversible; I shall return to this issue below.

As a rule, East European governments are obsessed with the issues of managing state-owned property and with the maximization of state revenues from property sales rather than with getting the privatization process going. The two exceptions are Eastern Germany and the ČSFR. In Germany, the major constraints of privatization are a less than expected interest on the part of West German investors to acquire East German properties, and a fairly low bureaucratic efficiency of the *Treuhandanstalt*. As regards the ČSFR, in 1991 the Czechoslovak government issued its decree on 'large-scale' privatization that affects several thousand state-owned enterprises;[23] in 1992, several hundred mutual funds were established and about 8.5 million vouchers were distributed among the population, and this got the privatization process going. However, as the evidence shows, only a handful of the mutual funds have an important role in the market for vouchers. Consequently, an immense concentration of ownership titles is occurring that will require a considerable effort by the successful mutual funds to manage their properties.

Most privatization plans list three criteria that can substantially limit the scope of privatization. First, the governments intend to retain the property rights of so-called 'strategic enterprises' or industries. For instance in Hungary, the government named about 160 state-owned enterprises that it considers to be companies of strategic importance. Within this group, the Hungarian government wants to retain the ownership rights either at the 100 per cent level, or at least with an absolute or relative majority holding. Such enterprises range from metallurgy and vehicle production through commercial banks and public utilities (such as the telecommunications company) to agricultural combines. In Poland, shipbuilding and coal mining, among others, are regarded as 'sensitive' industries.

Another aspect heavily emphasized by governments is the need to keep certain companies or industries in total or majority 'national ownership', the latter meaning a joint majority of state and domestic private owners. This endeavour usually has no rational economic

---

23 *Decree of the Government of the Czech and Slovak Federative Republic on the Disbursement and Usage of Investment Vouchers*, Prague, 5 September 1991.

basis, but it aims to appease significant groups of the population that loudly voice their objection to sell 'national treasures' to foreigners. Government bureaucracies in particular want to accommodate the opposition of political groups that are relatively close to the government. Finally, governments frequently emphasize their intention to upgrade and restructure the state-owned companies first and to sell them later. The governments' chief argument is that in several cases, enterprises to be sold have 'vast potential' that is not reflected in the initial offer prices, and in order to obtain a much higher price for these companies, they must be 'modernized'. There may be cases where such an argument is relevant. For instance, if an enterprise is not attractive enough to private investors because it carries old debts, or it has some units which are liabilities rather than assets and which can be detached easily, then an initial restructuring can improve the seller's bargaining position considerably. However, in most cases, restructuring would need a very long time and fresh capital – factors that the vast majority of the state-owned companies as well as the government lack the most. Therefore, playing for time would discourage private investors – especially foreign buyers – rather than provide the government with a bargaining chip. Consequently, in pursuit of maximizing short-term state revenues from privatization, the government would lose time and presumably more money than if it had privatized the enterprises swiftly and recovered its revenue from company taxes paid by the increasingly efficient private companies. Moreover, as was pointed out correctly by Åslund, it is not the revenues of the state but the capital inflow into the private sector that should be regarded as a 'progress indicator' of the privatization process.[24] (I return to this issue below in discussing the possible ways of privatization.)

Behind the governments' intentions and concerns mentioned above, there is another, but even more profound one. East European governments and the governing political parties often see privatization as a means of selecting and creating loyal supporters of their policies. Thus, privatization is envisaged as a process conducted on a discretionary individual basis, and the economic arguments are used to justify the ideological endeavours.

24 Åslund (1991a).

5.2.3 Different Groups of State-Owned Property

As regards the grouping of the state-owned property to be privatized, three different approaches can be identified. The most decisive one makes the distinction among groups of properties according to the different privatization techniques that are considered feasible and efficient for each group: industrial enterprises, agricultural land and cooperatives, the state-owned housing stock and the service companies or organizations. A second approach makes the distinction according to the size of the enterprises or other economic organizations to be privatized. From this angle, the very large – usually nationwide – monopolies, large-scale enterprises and small companies form separate groups. In some countries, such as Czechoslovakia, Hungary and Poland, a group of medium-sized companies is also distinguished, apart from the small-scale and the large enterprises. The medium-sized enterprises are regarded as large enough to stand out from the group of small companies, but they are not large enough to attract the government's permanent attention. Simplified procedures of privatization with some central control are envisaged by the government for this group of enterprises. (In the case of small-scale companies successive auctions are considered the most efficient route to privatization.)

Finally, a distinction is made between properties or enterprises whose output is marketable and those whose is not, or only to a limited extent. In other words, enterprises belonging to the competitive sector form a different group from those that belong to the non-competitive or regulated sectors. The most obvious examples for the latter case are the natural monopolies and public utilities with externality effects, for which privatization is envisaged – although only to a limited extent – on the supply side, but not on the demand side. Hence, East European governments are willing to offer concessions to private domestic or foreign companies to build and operate infrastructural facilities. Moreover, governments also intend to privatize, at least partially, some of the service enterprises; at the same time, the population's demand for services will be financed, in full or to a certain extent, from public sources.

5.2.4 The Speed of Privatization

One of the most fiercely debated issues of privatization within the East European governments and in political circles, and among economists, too, is how fast state ownership should be dismantled and turned into private ownership. At first glance, there is a mutual understanding among the economists in the East and West, shared by government officials, that privatization must be pursued 'as fast as possible'. However, the real issue is what is possible and feasible? For instance, Kornai – who himself is an advocate of radical privatization 'as fast as possible'[25] – asserts that 'Step-by-step changes are characteristic of the development of the private sector. It is impossible to institute private property by cavalry attack.'[26] Thus, Kornai considers the shift from a dominantly state-owned economy to an economy with dominant private ownership an organic and consequently time-consuming process. His main arguments cannot be ignored. Specifically, Kornai puts the emphasis on full liberalization of private businesses, and on the creation of institutions that guarantee the full legal security of the private sector. Moreover, he considers the emergence of a strong middle class to be an organic concomitant of privatization. Hence, the values, attitudes and behaviour of a private owner must take firm root in a decisive group of people alongside the development of legal and economic institutions. Finally, Kornai incorporates restructuring in the process of the private sector's birth.

Many East European economists and most East European governments (apart from Eastern Germany, for obvious reasons, and the Czechoslovak government, which has pursued a different approach) share Kornai's cautious and judicious views. However, the governments may have other reasons, at least in part, from those of Kornai for entertaining a gradualist approach. In particular, after a few months of 'honeymoon', the new East European governments face growing dissatisfaction and mistrust on the part of the population. They feel the basis of their power is frequently insecure. In some countries, such as in Bulgaria, Hungary, Poland and Romania, not to mention the republics of the former USSR, precious time has been wasted during the fight for political power among new political

25 Kornai (1990), p.80.
26 Ibid., p.54.

parties and pressure groups. Now East European governments consider the property rights of state enterprises as their last remaining asset. It is understandable, although a fairly short-sighted approach, if East European governments do not rush to dispose of 'their' properties, but try to use the re-allocation of property rights in order to strengthen their own power base.

As opposed to 'gradual–organic privatization', some Western economists – among them Olivier Blanchard and Richard Layard, Milton Friedman, David Lipton and Jeffrey Sachs, and Anders Åslund – as well as a few East European economists – including Václav Klaus and Dusan Triska in the ČSFR, and Attila K. Soós in Hungary – propose swift privatization accomplished within a few years. Allowing for some simplification, these authors interpret rapid privatization as the establishment of the 'rules of the game' of an economy dominated by private owners 'at once'. In addition, they want the state and its bureaucracies to be deprived of their property rights over a decisive majority of the national assets. These authors also recommend that the property rights be transferred to genuine private owners within a very short period of time (2 to 4 years). This transfer can partly be accomplished directly, but in part only indirectly, via new institutions (for example, 'privatization holding companies', 'mutual funds', etc.) that are entrusted by the ultimate owners to handle properties.

It is more or less clear that the advocates of rapid privatization make a firm distinction between the redefinition and re-allocation of property rights, on the one hand, and the restructuring of enterprises and other economic organizations, on the other, once the property rights of those companies have been transferred. Restructuring is envisaged by these authors as a long and painful process, since they consider the emergence of new social groups and classes a lengthy process as well. The distinction between privatization and restructuring is expressed in a more explicit way by Blanchard *et al.*,[27] but it is also mentioned by Lipton and Sachs, and by Åslund.[28]

What was not fully explored by the authors mentioned above are the interrelations between a swift change in property rights and the speedy formation of new institutions of private ownership, on the one

27 Blanchard *et al.* (1991).
28 Lipton and Sachs (1990), Åslund (1991b).

hand, and the role and impact of those institutions on the long process of restructuring, on the other. The links between the two processes are at least as crucial as the 'act' of privatization itself. Blanchard and Layard, and Lipton and Sachs (and also, for example, Janusz Lewandowski, the Polish Minister for Privatization) propose that the new forms of institutional private ownership (that is, privatization holding companies or mutual funds) should be set up by the state and subordinated to the government. These authors envisage that institutional owners would exist and take part in the restructuring for at least a decade. Consequently, the government's programme for privatization and restructuring must at least design a broad framework for these institutions' role in restructuring, just as it must set the limits of their authority. Moreover, it must be specified as clearly as possible in the government's programme how these institutions will be dissolved and their managers denied of the right to exploit their powerful position for their own benefit. Blanchard and Layard considered the legal (constitutional) safeguards written into the 'deed of foundation' of the privatization institutions sufficient to avoid 'unpleasant surprises'. However, their solution is fairly artificial and it ignores the new East European realities. Specifically, they regard the new East European governments as unchallenged repositories of authority to guarantee private property rights; however, in the light of East European developments during the past two or three years, we may have doubts about such a conviction.

Åslund does not think that the state or the government should actually create the new privatization institutions. These institutions may be formed by private - domestic and foreign - individuals.[29] While Åslund's proposition is more consistent than those described above, since it regards private agents as the most important and active participants of privatization and restructuring, whereas private actors are more or less 'passive observers' in Blanchard and Layard's conception, he presents the functions and operation of the privatization institutions in only general terms. Obviously, if the task of privatization and restructuring is left to private agents, a government programme for privatization cannot and must not describe (or prescribe) those agents' operations in detail. However, it is realistic to

29 Åslund (1991a).

say that the new private institutions cannot be left on their own from the outset. State institutions and private actors will be forced to cooperate intensively until the private sector gains sufficient strength. Moreover, as time goes by and more experience accumulates, the 'constitutional rules' covering property rights may need greater or lesser adjustments. It is the state's responsibility to initiate these adjustments. Finally, the state may – and, as evidence shows, in fact will – remain a co-owner, even if only a minority owner, of the national assets; consequently, the state bureaucracy will have a say in restructuring as well. It is much better to address this issue at an early stage of privatization rather than leave it to endless disputes later. I discuss the feedbacks between privatization and restructuring in final Chapter 6 below.

If all the authors mentioned above advocate rapid privatization, and their proposals are similar in most respects when it comes to the technical details, why do their views still differ as regards the role of the state (government) and private agents? It is my impression that Western economists' approaches diverge because of their slightly different picture of the past communist regimes and on the present state of the East European countries. Thus, Lipton and Sachs, and Blanchard and Layard, take it for granted that there exist considerable social forces in Eastern Europe that are determined to move unambiguously towards a Western-type market economy and political democracy. On the other hand, these authors consider the remains of the old communist *nomenklatura* to be the most decisive and powerful opponents of the economic and political changes in an 'indirect way'. Specifically, these Western economists argue that by having fostered 'spontaneous privatization' the old *nomenklatura* has become the largest beneficiary of the economic transformation so far. Thus, the opposition to radical systemic changes among large social groups is, or can be, fuelled chiefly by these people's anger, since they feel they have been cheated. To be fair, both pairs of authors emphasize that a potential backlash can occur in economic transformation if workers' resistance to growing unemployment and diminishing living standards gathers momentum. Hence, these authors favour rapid privatization in order to put a leash on 'spontaneous privatization' by the old *nomenklatura* and to accomplish a systemic transformation before popular resistance and open unrest become

unmanageable. Consequently, the new, democratically elected governments, with the obvious support of the majority of the electorate, can
and must be the chief players in the economic transformation for
many years to come. In the light of the experience of East European
transitions so far, and especially on the basis of the national and local
election results in Poland at the end of October 1991, the above line
of reasoning can hardly be sustained.[30]

Other Western economists, such as, for example, Anders Åslund,
share most of the ideas mentioned above, but they preserve at least
some reservation about the intentions of the new East European state
bureaucracies and governments. They sense the danger of the possible
emergence of extreme populist regimes and new dictators (mainly in
the republics of the disintegrating Soviet Union) to a certain degree.[31]
However, sometimes the same Western analysts entertain the idea that
a strong leader who is personally committed to radical changes may
navigate economic transformation in the right direction. (Time and
again, this is the case with Boris Yeltsin, as it was, at least until
recently, with Polish president Lech Wałęsa.)

It is important to note that East European countries differ to a
considerable extent as regards the development level of their
economic institutions (including the private sector), the level of their
democratic institutions, and their popular traditions and experience
with Western-type market economies. Consequently, what can be
regarded as an intolerable degree of state interventionism in one
country with a fairly developed institutional system of the market
economy (for example, in Hungary) may well be necessary assistance
from the state to the private sector in its embryonic stage (for
example, in Bulgaria, Romania and the former USSR). Moreover,
while state intervention may unnecessarily curtail the autonomy of the
economic agents and slow down economic adjustment and stabilization in an economy with smaller imbalances, a resolute government
policy for stabilization may be unavoidable in a country that is on the
verge of total economic collapse. Nevertheless, it appears impossible
to achieve a successful and swift economic transformation from the

30 See above, p.61, n.10. Even more strikingly, the Party of Democratic Socialism - the
heir of the communist party - won the national elections in Lithuania in November
1992.
31 See, for example, *Dagens Nyheter*, 27 October 1991.

command economy to a market economy with dominant private ownership if the transformation is chiefly designed and conducted by state bureaucracies. Although mathematical models of privatization mentioned earlier[32] convincingly argue that 'speed is almost everything', this is true only if we disregard all the other factors relevant to privatization – and constraints upon the process – that have been discussed above.

5.2.5 How can Privatization be Accomplished?

East European governments apply different privatization methods to different types of state-owned property. In fact, the initially vague measures and methods have now congealed as a 'plan for a diversified approach' to privatization in most countries. Thus, it is generally accepted by the East European governments that leasing out and auctioning off small-scale businesses, such as restaurants, retail trade shops and other local service units, are the most reasonable methods of privatizing this part of the state-owned assets. There is a considerable difference among East European governments, though, when it comes to the practical execution of small-scale privatization. Thus, leasing out and auctioning off was completely decentralized to local government in the ČSFR, and it was reasonably decentralized in the former GDR and Poland, too. However, for instance in Hungary, auctions were organized and administered by a directorate of the State Property Agency (SPA). In addition, the SPA was authorized to set the initial bidding price for each individual piece of property (say, a restaurant or grocery store). The different approaches of the Czechoslovak, German and Polish governments, on the one hand, and the Hungarian, on the other, are well reflected in the actual results of small privatization so far: namely, most restaurants, retail trade shops and local service companies were turned over to private hands in the first three countries, while at the same time, the Hungarian government first reduced the number of enterprises and service units to be privatized from 12,000 to 4,000, then the SPA managed to conclude only about 1,000 small privatization agreements by the end of 1991.[33] (It must be added that the starting conditions for a

32 Roland and Verdier (1991), and Laban and Wolf (1991).

small-scale private sector were much more favourable in Hungary than in the other East European countries – with the exception, perhaps, of Poland – since several thousand shops and restaurants and other private businesses had been leased out to or were owned by private entrepreneurs.) In 1992, small privatization accelerated in Hungary, and the SPA auctioned off another 4,000 business units.[34]

As a general rule, the ownership of apartments formerly owned by the state (in practice by the local councils) is being transferred to the tenants of these apartments in all East European countries. The details of the ownership transfer may reveal some important differences again among the East European countries. It can be observed that in countries where rents on state-owned apartments were artificially low and both the structure of municipalities and their new legal regulation are modestly developed, the transfer of ownership progressed faster than in countries with more sophisticated regulation and more realistic prices for dwelling space. (The ČSFR may be a good example of the former case, with the former GDR and Hungary for the latter.) In Eastern Germany, the issue of housing ownership is further complicated by the German government's willingness to allow for reprivatization of apartment houses on a large scale. In Hungary, the property rights of the apartment stock were first transferred to the local governments, and the municipal authorities can now decide how they want to privatize the apartments. These bodies frequently consider real estate as a major source of local revenue, so many of them are unwilling to dispose of properties at a low price. Other local governments want to create their own private companies based on the real estate owned by themselves. Consequently, privatization of state-owned apartments is not always as easy as it might seem.

Privatization of agricultural land is a 'hot potato' in most East European countries, apart from Poland. (In Poland, more than 70 per cent of the arable agricultural land has been privately owned as a matter of tradition.) This is a type of property whose reprivatization and restitution are strongly demanded by influential political groups in most countries: restitution of agricultural land is planned in Bulgaria, the ČSFR, the former GDR, Hungary and Romania.

33 *Heti Világgazdaság*, 16 November 1991.
34 *Privinfo*, Vol.I, No.12, 1992.

In Hungary, a very complex system of restitution was elaborated by the government and it was endorsed by parliament in April 1991.[35] According to the law, physical restitution of agricultural land can be claimed by the original owner or its heirs up to a certain size of the lost land. However, it is not guaranteed by the law that every original owner will automatically receive his or her lost parcel of land. Original owners will get 'compensation vouchers' and they can bid for an actual spot of agricultural land with their vouchers. Above a certain value limit, financial compensation will apply to every original owner, according to a regressive scale. In 1992, the Hungarian government decided that the compensated original owners could convert their compensation vouchers into securities of selected state-owned companies. In addition, compensation vouchers may be exchanged for securities of the commercial banks that are to be privatized. Finally, vouchers may be used to buy certain consumer goods in the stores of some retail trade companies, or they can be sold to private investment funds and traded on the Budapest stock exchange.

In Albania, restitution is mixed with free distribution of property in the form of land.[36] In the former USSR, a lease-out of agricultural land has already started, and distribution of land to peasants may come later in the republics. As regards the Baltic states, they seem to long for restitution, too.

It is not exclusively agricultural land, but other sorts of confiscated real estate as well, that is planned to be restored or compensated for by the East European governments. An outstanding issue of restitution is the reprivatization of religious properties. It is common knowledge that different churches and religious life at large were oppressed or at least severely constrained in each East European country. Churches were deprived of most of their properties and revenues from those properties, and they were kept on a 'short leash' by the state budget. In addition, communist states tightly controlled the personnel policy of the churches: notably, the appointment of priests – especially to higher religious positions – had to be approved by the communist party and state authorities. Consequently, it goes without saying that the freedom of religion cannot be restored in Eastern Europe without

35 Okolicsanyi (1991).
36 Åslund and Sjöberg (1991).

securing the legal and economic autonomy of different churches. But how should this autonomy be created?

In order to answer the above question, the issue of coexistence between a democratic state and the churches must be addressed first. If religion and religious life are envisaged as a form of individual liberty and the right of assembly, then a logical solution is that state and churches should be separated. In that case, an extensive programme of restitution of religious properties is not the direction to take. After all, a large-scale restitution serves to restore wealth, but also effectively restores a political-cultural role that churches played before the communist era. As is well known, churches had been an important and organic part of the political state in most East European countries before the Second World War, or under the Tsarist regime in Russia and other member republics of the former USSR. Religious leaders and their churches had considerable political power and influence on most policy matters beyond the directly religious ones. Churches and state institutions had been deeply intertwined, in a similar way, although perhaps to a lesser degree, to how the communist parties and state bureaucracies were. As the revival of different churches flourishes in Eastern Europe, we have every reason to observe that the restitution of religious properties is being encouraged not only by the churches but also by powerful political parties and groups that also serve the cause of restoring the churches' social position. And, paradoxical as it may sound, the march for more power and for a larger share of the national wealth is led in many cases by church leaders who had been promoted to their current positions by the communist authorities, many of whom had also served as agents of the secret police. Since legal institutions of a political democracy, and especially the democratic representation of different social groups, are not fully developed in the East European countries (to put it in a low-key and optimistic manner), too much is left to the sobriety and restraint of religious leaders and too little rests with the interests and institutions of a democratic society.

Finally, a partial financial compensation for small businesses that had been confiscated by the communist regimes, or a full restitution in kind, is planned in most East European countries as well.

In terms of complexity, the most difficult and important issue in East European privatization concerns medium-scale and large-scale state-owned industrial enterprises. This is the very issue that can have the most decisive impact on the East European countries' future economic development and on their possible reintegration into an advanced world economy. In the light of this, East European governments and economists devote less than adequate attention to the issues of so-called 'large privatization'. Moreover, the progress of actual privatization has been fairly modest on this count, as will be discussed below.

There are too many issues regarding large-scale privatization to render feasible an exhaustive discussion of them all. A first and obvious issue is whether East European privatizations should use the conventional methods of property sales applied by advanced Western countries? Or do they rather need new, untried solutions? As a matter of policy, it must be – or rather should have been – decided by the East European governments and parliaments if foreign buyers of state-owned properties were to be favoured in order to complete a first round of privatizations as fast as possible, or whether domestic private owners should have priority in the privatization process. Or, can and must a reasonable balance between the two be established? As I showed above, disposable savings of the East European populations cannot match the sales value of the state-owned property, provided that sales of property at a realistic market price are considered the desirable solution. Consequently, the large-scale and rapid sale of state-owned properties almost automatically favours foreign buyers. However, if East European parliaments intend to favour domestic private owners, it means either a drastic reduction of the properties' sales price and additional financial support to domestic buyers from the government by granting preferential loans, or some form of free distribution of the state-owned property.

Thirdly, East European governments must sort out the issues of privatization and those of restructuring. In particular, they must make clear whether privatization is envisaged as a comprehensive change in the system of property rights, and that alone, or whether it is intended to solve as well the strategic issues of restructuring industries and individual enterprises. Obviously, these two aspects cannot always be completely disentangled. But East European governments must make a policy decision, at least, about whether they intend to involve state organizations in the reshaping of domestic industries – or in only some of those industries - or whether they want to leave this task completely to the new owners.

In addition, privatization in Eastern Europe is almost always accompanied by the immediate closing down of parts of enterprises and ensuing unemployment of the companies' staff. Governments must take an unambiguous stand on whether any likely unemployment connected with privatization should be regarded as a factor inherent in privatization strategies and individual decisions, or whether privatization and unemployment should be separated as far as possible. Should the government choose the latter option, it must have a comprehensive programme of tackling unemployment and assisting in retraining. Such a programme must include a plan to upgrade services as well, since in many cases poorly developed transport facilities, telecommunications and housing prevent the unemployed from seeking vacancies in regions other than where they live.[37] Numerous other problems might have been mentioned above. Instead of listing them all, I shall discuss only a few that I consider to be the most crucial. First, I describe the different ways of large privatization as envisaged and actually practised in the East European countries. Secondly, and closely connected with that issue, I discuss the role of foreign investors and advisers in the privatization process. Thirdly, I focus on the interrelations between privatization and state finances. Finally, I outline some implications of privatization for the restructuring of East European companies and industries.

Privatization methods

Whereas 'large privatization' is seen by East European governments as only one, although very important, aspect of a diversified and complex process that aims at transforming the system of property rights, the privatization of larger state-owned enterprises is envisaged as a multiple approach in itself. There is only one factor that unifies the different ways of large privatization: the ultimate seller of the properties (thus, the representative of the original owner, that is, the state) must always be a state organization. In each country, a special agency (for example, in the ČSFR a department of the Ministry of Finance, in Germany the *Treuhandanstalt*, in Hungary the State

---

37 I discussed these issues in Major (1991d).

Property Agency and since July 1992 also the State Holding Company, in Poland the Ministry of Ownership Transformation originally, and since early 1991 the Ministry of Privatization) have been entitled to represent the state as owner and seller. Moreover, these agencies were assigned to do the operative work concerning every privatization deal. These state agencies have grown into fairly large bureaucracies with enormous power over the enterprises. Besides the property agencies, other state offices, such as the branch ministries, also have a say in specific privatization deals, but their influence is usually limited.

Another general remedy cherished by the East European governments to overcome the practical barriers of privatization is to initiate privatization by converting the state-owned enterprises into joint stock companies. (This conversion is called 'corporatization' or 'commercialization' in Eastern Europe.) However, because of the lack of a well-functioning capital market (including a stock exchange), enterprise conversions usually aim at creating a closed shareholding company with a severely restricted number of shareholders. Furthermore, most of the shareholders are themselves state organizations, such as the state property agency, state-owned commercial banks that keep the enterprise's account – and carry its debt – and other state-owned companies that have organic business contacts with the given enterprise. Then, 'real' privatization is considered through an attempt to sell off a share of the property agency's stake in the enterprise to outside buyers.

Most East European governments regard case-by-case sales of the state-owned enterprises as the main road towards the transformation of property rights. The actual methods used in these sales show great variety. The most frequently used solution is to launch an initial public offering (IPO) of an enterprise. The IPO can be organized in the framework of an open tender, or through a tender among invited potential buyers. Or it can turn into an attempt to secure an outright sale to a pre-selected buyer. One of the critical aspects of an IPO is, who selects the potential buyers and according to what criteria are the buyers selected? Usually, the initiative for privatization comes from an enterprise itself. On numerous occasions, the enterprise managers come forward with a specific proposal about their buyer. In countries such as Hungary and Poland, and the ČSFR to a lesser extent, where state-owned enterprises have had fairly extensive foreign trade contacts and, above all, licensing agreements with foreign partners, such a proposal may be well-founded. However, state agencies want to preserve an image of 'neutrality' and to convince the public that their only concern is to represent the 'interests of the nation as a whole'. Consequently, they present other proposals, or they immediately decide to begin the enterprise's privatization by issuing a call for tenders by any interested party. In addition, domestic or foreign investors others than those who had been proposed by the enterprise itself may directly approach the state agency with an offer.[38] Sometimes, but by no means exceptionally, these 'back-door' offers are supported, at least discreetly, by influential political groups, party leaders or members of the government. Then, a 'fair contest' is launched by the state agency among the interested partners. The IPO is regarded as a mainstream of privatization in Germany and Hungary: for instance in Hungary, the government expects that the IPO will account for about 40–50 per cent of all privatization deals.[39]

After having realized the clumsiness of the centrally administered privatization deals, state agencies, above all the German _Treuhand_[40] and the Hungarian SPA, started entertaining the idea of leveraged management buy-outs (LMBOs). In this case, the managers of a certain enterprise are supposed to come forward with a proposal for privatization and restructuring of their own company. In addition, they must be willing to invest their own resources into the company and borrow the rest of the sale price from banks. Then the state agency sets the initial sale price for the enterprise and it acts as a controlling body of the privatization process. The state agency may also require that an independent (mostly private) advising agency should be involved in the privatization, supposedly to assist the state agency as well as the potential buyers throughout the whole process. In Hungary, the LMBO is thought of by the government as a method

38 I discussed the three different legal ways of initiating the privatization of a large state-owned enterprise in Hungary in Major (1991b).

39 'Javaslat a Kormány tulajdonosi és privatizációs stratégiájára (4. változat).' (Recommendations for the government's strategy of ownership and privatization. Version 4), Ministry of Finance, Budapest, July 1991, and _Figyelő_, 10 October 1991.

40 A highly critical assessment of the _Treuhandanstalt_'s activities so far was outlined in _The Economist_, 14 September 1991, pp.21–4, and in the _Financial Times_, 9 September 1991.

that will gain more and more weight among the different options of privatization in the near future. Thus, the LMBO may account for 20–30 per cent of the privatized property in value terms.[41]

A third method is a leveraged buy-out of a share of the enterprise's assets by its own employees. This method is chiefly used as a complementary and subordinated device to other forms of privatization. This method is called the 'employee stock ownership plan' (ESOP), as it was named in the USA, whereby employees of an enterprise acquire usually a minority stake in the assets at a preferential price; in addition, they can take out cheap loans to cover their purchases of shares. In most East European countries, the ESOP is envisaged as a method that may take up at most 10–20 per cent of the assets.[42]

Finally, for smaller-sized state-owned enterprises a so-called 'simplified procedure of privatization' is designed by governments. In this case, the enterprise management is free to open negotiations with potential buyers and it can choose a privatization adviser from a list of advising agencies previously endorsed by the state property agency. This method has already been introduced in Hungary. In the first round, 437 enterprises were selected for the 'self-privatization' programme.[43] The second group of another 278 companies started in May 1992. In the second phase, companies whose assets have a book value of less than one billion forints may choose the method of self-privatization.[44] Some variant of the method may well also be applied soon in Poland and the ČSFR.

A different approach is applied to nationwide monopolies or public utilities that East European governments intend to privatize in part. As an initial step, governments usually convert these economic organizations also into joint stock companies; however, the only shareholder of such a company is the state, perhaps a state-owned bank. Here, as a rule, an IPO is launched next as an offer to pre-selected potential

41 Ibid.
42 For Hungary, see references under footnote 39; for Poland, see 'Privatization in Poland: Program and Achievements', Ministry of Privatization (Warsaw, August 1991), and 'Sprawozdanie z realizacji uchwaly Sejmu z 23.02.1991 r.; W Sprawie podstawowych kierunków prywatyzacji w 1991 r.; Wraz z ocena efektów finansowych prywatyzacji w I polroczu 1991 r.; Oraz wnioskami dokonania korekt kierunków prywatyzacji', Warsaw, 1991.
43 See *Napi Világgazdaság*, 8 October 1991; and *Világgazdaság*, 24 October 1991.
44 *Figyelő*, 9 April 1992, and *Heti Világgazdaság*, 26 December 1992.

rule, an IPO is launched next as an offer to pre-selected potential buyers. Moreover, privatization, that is, selling a share of the company's assets, is combined with, or preceded by, a concessionary offer to would-be outside investors. In general, the future structure of shareholders is envisaged as one where the state retains its absolute majority among the owners of such a company's assets.

In Albania, the ČSFR, Poland and Romania, the state authorities have already endorsed, or they plan to implement, a radically different way of privatization from the ones mentioned above: namely, the free distribution of a considerable part of the state-owned property as a break-through method of privatization. In Albania, apart from agricultural land and small-scale businesses, an extensive free distribution of the property rights of state-owned enterprises to citizens and employees is proposed by the government.[45] In Czechoslovakia, 44 per cent of the total assets of 1,435 state-owned enterprises in the Czech Republic, and 62 per cent of the assets of 573 state-owned enterprises in the Slovak Republic are planned to be 'sold' against vouchers that are distributed among the whole population for a nominal registration fee. (The total book value of state-owned enterprises to be privatized is Kčs 378 bn in the Czech Republic, and Kčs 141 bn in the Slovak Republic.)[46]

In Poland, successive plans for such a free distribution surfaced during 1990-92.[47] Therefore, it is hard to tell what the 'really existing' privatization programme of the Polish government is. A comprehensive version of the programme for privatization that had been elaborated by the Ministry of Privatization (headed by Janusz Lewandowski) before the national elections of 26 October 1991, envisaged the free distribution of a 60 per cent share in more than 400 large state-owned enterprises. (Another 30 per cent of the enterprise's assets was planned to be allocated to the Treasury, and 10 per cent to the employees of the enterprises.) More precisely, these enterprises would have been - and some of them already had been - converted into joint stock companies first ('commercialization'), after which

45 See Åslund and Sjöberg (1991).
46 See, for example, *Financial Times*, 9 October 1991, and *Reuter* (*Világgazdaság*, 8 November 1991); on the legal regulation of privatization via vouchers see '*Decree of the Government of the Czech and Slovak Federative Republic ...*', op. cit.
47 See, for example, *Rzeczpospolita*, 3 August 1991, and a critique of this version by Marcin Swiecicki in *Gazeta Wyborcza*, No.148, 8 August 1991.

shares in these companies would have been given to mutual funds set up by the Polish government, and headed by government-appointed domestic and foreign managers; between five and twenty such mutual funds were to have been created in the first round. Finally, shares in the newly established mutual funds would have been distributed among all adult Polish citizens.[48]

Since the launch of the latest version of this plan the number of enterprises to be included in the free distribution package has been gradually reduced to 205. And after the national election of 1991, Minister Lewandowski made a statement that privatization at large must be slowed down and a more cautious approach pursued. There were several reasons for taking a more gradualist stand. One was the opposition on the part of the enterprise councils and the trade unions to rapid privatization, entailing the full or partial liquidation of companies and the ensuing dismissal of employees on a large scale. Another heavyweight argument was the organizational and bureaucratic inability of the state institutions, above all the Ministry of Privatization, to handle mass privatization properly.[49] However, during the course of 1992, it was the complete chaos of the Polish political and governmental structure rather than technical problems of administering privatization that prevented Poland from making progress in the privatization process. During the second half of 1992, however, the Suchocka government and Privatization Minister Lewandowski (who returned to this office after a few months of intermission) succeeded in accelerating privatization through the liquidation of the state-owned enterprises. But the free distribution scheme, and especially the setting up of the privatization holdings with foreign participation, is still on hold in Poland.

In Romania, the parliament passed a law on privatization in August 1991. According to this Act, 30 per cent of the state-owned enterprises' assets will be distributed to the adult citizens of the country through mutual funds. The programme for free distribution was designed by the government with the assistance of the British accountancy and investment consulting company, Coopers & Lybrand.[50] In the former Soviet Union, an 'Act on the Initial Phase of

48 See 'Privatization in Poland. Program and Achievements', op. cit.
49 *Finance Eastern Europe (The Financial Times)*, Vol.1, No.17, 23 October 1991.
50 *Financial Times*, 17 October 1991.

Denationalization and Privatization of Enterprises' was adopted by the Congress of People's Deputies in August 1991.[51] However, the coup swept away the cautious plans for privatization, and very soon the disintegration of the USSR followed. In 1992 a voucher scheme, or other forms of free distribution, were under consideration by some former member republics of the USSR, such as Lithuania and Russia. The programme of the Russian government of October 1991, made public as the 'Yeltsin Programme', already included directives for comprehensive and rapid privatization, but it was short of details.[52] A more comprehensive and detailed three-year plan for stabilization and privatization was submitted by the Gaidar government in June 1992, which unambiguously opted for a large-scale free distribution of state-owned property.[53] In November 1992, an ambitious plan for this was announced by the Gaidar government; however, by the end of December Prime Minister Yegor Gaidar had been replaced by Viktor Chernomyrdin, who is considered a representative of the military-industrial complex. It is doubtful – to put it no higher – whether the new prime minister will follow the path of privatization selected by his predecessor, although formally the free distribution of state-owned properties is on the political agenda of the Russian and also of several other East European governments.

Free distribution is strongly supported by numerous Western economists, including, for example, Milton Friedman, David Lipton and Jeffrey Sachs, Olivier Blanchard and Richard Layard, and Anders Åslund, but it is bluntly rejected by quite a few others. The best-known opponent of free distribution is János Kornai. An important argument of those who favour free distribution is that this method of privatization is fair to the general public, as opposed to other, discretionary methods that automatically favour one group of citizens or another. (The authors mentioned above point out that members of the old *nomenklatura* and black marketeers can take the greatest benefit from the case-by-case sale of state-owned property.) The opponents of a property give-away reverse this argument, asserting that an equal distribution of state-owned assets can be

51 *Izvestiya*, 8 August 1991.
52 See *Sovetskaya Rossiya*, 29 October 1991.
53 *Financial Times*, 1 July 1992. On the privatization programmes of the CIS countries see also Frydman *et al.* (1993b).

extremely unjust, to the detriment of the hard-working and inventive would-be entrepreneurs and to the advantage of the 'below average' achievers.

A positive critique of free distribution was formulated by Kornai. First, he argued that most beneficiaries of a free distribution would regard their share from the distributed property as an unexpected gift or a bequest left to them by 'Daddy state' who had passed away.[54] Then, the vast majority of the heirs would rush to make a quick revenue out of their inheritance. This move would not contribute to the emergence of private owners in a great number, while it would certainly add a large boost to inflation and it might also aggravate shortages. Secondly, Kornai elaborated in detail an organic way of creating a market economy with dominant private ownership. He pointed out that selling state-owned properties to private buyers for a realistic price is an organic element of establishing markets, including capital markets, and it is also a factor crucial to the formation of sound, market-compatible attitudes and behaviour on the part of private economic agents.[55]

Kornai made a number of relevant points regarding different aspects of privatization. However, he avoided facing the problems that emerge from an organic and inevitably gradual – and consequently fairly slow – process of the transformation of property rights, the very aspect that the advocates of a free distribution emphasize the most. Notably, they argue that East European countries have no time to waste if they want to gain the broad support of their own populations for the painful but unavoidable steps of the transition. According to Lipton and Sachs, if Poland, or any other East European country for that matter, chooses a gradual approach to privatization, '... the political battle over privatization will soon lead to a stalemate in the entire process, with the devastating long-term result that little privatization takes place at all.'[56] I shall argue in detail in the next

54 Kornai (1990), pp.81-2.
55 Since the publication of his book in 1990, Kornai has modified his views to some extent. In particular, while he still argues in favour of an evolutionary road towards dominant private ownership, he is willing to accept free distribution of state-owned property to non-profit institutions, educational and philanthropic organizations, Churches and foundations. Kornai revealed these ideas in his *Tinbergen Lecture* (held in the Netherlands on 19 October 1990): see Kornai (1991), p.1038.
56 Lipton and Sachs (1990), pp.297-8.

chapter that both Kornai and advocates of a free distribution of
state-owned properties on a mass scale extend their arguments too far,
while neglecting or omitting crucial aspects of privatization in Eastern
Europe. These include, for instance, the genuine endeavours and
attitudes of large social groups towards privatization, a thorough
analysis of the issues of restructuring related to privatization, the
impact of 'scarce resources' in the form of organizational, administrative and bureaucratic capacities and bureaucratic efficiency in general
in Eastern Europe, and finally, a deep understanding of the new
political forces and state institutions that are emerging in these
countries.

The envisaged role of foreign investors and advisers

After a very short period between 1918 and 1921, when Lenin made
some efforts to attract foreign investors in the West (he proposed that
foreigners should acquire concessions in Soviet Russia), and again
between 1945 and 1948, when East European governments designed
development plans that included extensive direct foreign investment
in their countries, the presence of Western investors was a rare
exception rather than a common practice in Eastern Europe. (The
former GDR provided limited concessions to West Germany in West
Berlin; moreover, 'joint ventures' of Soviet and domestic East
European state-owned enterprises were established on a large scale
after the Second World War, but these companies could hardly be
considered genuine business ventures.) Even those very few Western
investments that did occur had been licensed outside the prevailing
formal legal regulations. It was not until the late 1980s that various
East European central authorities began to show a growing concern
about foreign direct investment and the related legal issues of
property rights.

Since then, the role, the potential economic gains and losses, and
the legal aspects of foreign direct investment and property acquisition,
have become the most popular topics of discussions in the East
European countries. Exaggerated hopes have been nurtured regarding
an immediate enrichment of the countries concerned along with
irrationally extreme fears that foreigners would 'bleed our country
white' and then run off with the profits. East European governments
have tried to find a 'golden mean' between these two extremes. For

instance, in Hungary the government is willing to accept a maximum of 25–30 per cent share of foreign ownership (it is not yet clear what the basis of reference for those figures is). In Poland, reservations directed against foreign investors are greater in the context of public statements, but government offices are doing their best to attract as much foreign investment as possible. A similar story can be told about the other East European countries as well. In fact, a 'siege' of East European countries by foreign investors offers far fewer grounds for concern than does the lack of Western investors' resolve to start business in these countries, as I shall argue below.

The East European countries' expectations towards Western investors include a massive inflow of modern technologies, an injection of advanced organizational, managerial and marketing skills and know-how into the ailing industries and a decisive inflow of cash in convertible currencies and finance capital. In addition, East European governments also hope that foreign owners will contribute to the emergence of a healthy ownership structure in these countries. Consequently, state bureaucracies favour large, 'serious' investors (possibly multinationals), and they try to scare away 'sparrow-hawk' small investors. (This expression was coined by a Hungarian deputy from the largest governing party in 1990, and he used it publicly several times on Hungarian television.)

There is another reason why state agencies favour large investors over smaller ones: namely, that it appears easier from a bureaucratic point of view to negotiate with a few dozen large potential buyers than with hundreds or thousands of small businessmen. Moreover, the financial standing and credibility of large foreign companies can be checked more easily by East European officials than the standing and reputation of small businessmen. Last but not least, since privatization is very much centralized in each East European country, government attitudes and practices towards privatization have begun to resemble previous practices of fulfilling central plans. Thus, it is easier to fulfil a government's privatization plan by selling off state-owned enterprises – or rather a share of those enterprises – to a smaller number of 'wholesale' investors rather than bothering about several 'retailers' and trying to sell enterprises one by one.

If not in principle, then certainly in reality, selling enterprises or parts of enterprises to foreign buyers is regarded by East European governments and property agencies as constituting 'real' privatization of state-owned property. Contrary to the fine-sounding principles concerning direct foreign investment, property agencies and governments pursue a very pragmatic policy in this respect. The keyword is simple: 'Sell everything!' In reality, however, property acquisitions by foreigners do not always run their course so smoothly. Apart from different aims pursued by foreigners during the acquisition process – endeavours that are not always accepted as fair – foreign investors are confronted with often contradictory requirements of the East European governments and other state agencies. Such controversial issues occur when a government wants to receive guarantees from the potential buyer concerning the future restructuring of an enterprise, but the same government then tries to impose restrictions on the foreign owner's personnel policy, and especially regarding dismissals. Another controversial issue is the sale price of enterprises in relation to non-negligible enterprise debts. Foreigners naturally want to buy an enterprise without any accompanying liabilities, while sellers try to sell at least a part of the company's debt along with the assets. A third, and increasingly important, issue are the unforeseen environmental costs directly connected to a company's operation. Foreign investors have begun to worry that they are purchasing enormous but undetected environmental liabilities when they buy an East European company. The reverse of the coin is that some multinational or foreign companies try to 'export' their polluting production lines to Eastern Europe, after those manufacturing activities had been banned in their home countries.

When East European governments decided to open up their countries to foreign investors in the late 1980s and early 1990s, they tried to attract foreigners by offering generous tax concessions for joint ventures with foreign participation. In fact, a peculiar race started among East European countries regarding the level and duration of tax privileges offered to foreigners. However, evidence showed that foreign private investors with long-term investment plans were much less sensitive to the tax concessions than to macro-economic and political stability, to the security of their profits and invested capital, to the level of development of financial services and infrastructure, and to the degree of bureaucratic constraints on establishing companies and engaging in foreign trade.

Several Western and East European economists have also argued that East European countries should replace their domestic currencies with a convertible currency because the lack of currency convertibility prevents foreigners from investing. Thus, Poland, the ČSFR and Romania have already declared their currencies convertible and Russia and other republics of the former USSR plan to do the same. Hungary meanwhile has refrained from declaring the convertibility of the forint; nevertheless, that country has managed to attract about 50 per cent of all foreign direct investment in Eastern Europe in the two and a half years from mid-1990. Hence, formal convertibility of the East European currencies – although desirable, provided that the necessary conditions of convertibility are met and convertibility can be sustained – does not seem to be an inevitable precondition of substantial inflow of foreign direct investment.[57]

What can become a much more serious barrier to foreign direct investment than the lack of currency convertibility is an unrealistic exchange rate regime. This danger is far from hypothetical in Eastern Europe, where the exchange rate is regulated centrally and it does not always conform to changes in the domestic price level. Since the rate of inflation has been high in all East European countries, a growing gap has developed between domestic inflation and the inflation rate of the East European countries' most important trading partners. Consequently, the countries' domestic currency has appreciated almost automatically against the convertible currencies, which made East European exports less and less lucrative. But Western investors – especially the multinational companies – found the local markets too small and too risky and they lost interest in East European joint ventures as those companies were less and less able to export at a competitive price. The multinational companies' first reaction was to demand of the governments large-scale devaluation of the domestic currency against hard currencies. But East European governments were reluctant to devalue the local currency because devaluation proved to be a short-term remedy for the the weakening export incentives, while it fuelled inflation. Consequently, the exchange rate of the East European currencies became a very controversial issue between potential foreign investors and East European governments.

57 See, for example, Blue Ribbon Commission (1992).

Several other problems regarding property acquisitions could be mentioned, including the rights of each co-owner in cases where a foreign investor remains a minority owner after the acquisition, or the rights of, and limitations on, the state as an owner in a company with foreign participation, the role of banks and the currency regulations that apply to different types of joint ventures, and so on. Be that as it may, foreign acquisitions today shape privatization in the sector of large state-owned enterprises in most East European countries.

At the present stage, the role of foreign advisory agencies has become a very important issue in Eastern Europe. These agencies were originally private companies providing services of accountancy, investment consultancy and legal assistance and operating in several Western countries. If East European governments want to sell enterprises to foreign buyers, they need to undertake a thorough evaluation of enterprise assets that meets Western standards. Moreover, East European enterprises and state property agencies are in need of assistance during the process of searching for interested buyers. Finally, expert help, provided by Western investment banks and accountancy companies, cannot hurt when it comes to negotiations with potential foreign investors. Most of the Western advisory agencies have extensive expertise in conventional case-by-case privatization, and on LMBOs, mergers and other forms of sophisticated operations on Western capital markets. In addition to that asset, they have widespread contacts with Western companies that can be approached with offers. But above all, Western advisory agencies are private companies themselves that seek every single opportunity to earn profits and obtain a share of the market. What is not always so obvious as their merits enumerated above is their knowledge of and interest in the local conditions, historical development and current needs of the East European economies.

As a point of departure, Western advisory agencies have usually been invited and licensed by the state authorities. These companies had no previous contacts, or only very limited ones, with East European enterprises. As the evidence shows, Western advisory agencies became in the first place the partners of state agencies responsible for privatization, and they are involved in the enterprises' burning problems only to a much lesser extent. The lack, on the one hand, of a vision of future property rights on the part of East

European governments – or the presence of such a vision in only a fragmented form – and the absence of a clear programme of privatization, coupled with an almost magnetic challenge and the bright prospects of easy profits, on the other hand, has landed Western advisory agencies in a situation of some controversy.

I wish to emphasize that I fully acknowledge and respect the outstanding expertise and accumulated knowledge of Western investment banks and accountancy firms. I am also convinced that these banks and companies could have a decisive role in the East European privatization, a role, moreover, that could be more fruitful for the East European countries and lucrative to Western advisers, too. I shall discuss an alternative to the current utilization of Western advising agencies in the next chapter. For the moment I wish simply to point out that, while private advising agencies are interested – because they are made interested – in being paid properly by the East European state agencies and in selling off state-owned enterprises for a price that is acceptable to the government, they are not particularly concerned to help accelerate the privatization process. In addition, they have very little interest in finding outside investors in East European companies who will then make strategic decisions about their newly acquired properties. Rather, their interest in the future of the privatized companies is optional and left to personal ambitions at best. And finally, the advising agencies themselves are not supposed to be concerned about the long-term issues of the restructuring and reintegrating of East European companies into the advanced world economy. We may conclude that foreign acquisitions and foreign assistance to East European privatization measures are considered by East European governments as decisive contributors to economic transformation, and foreign participation should be regarded even more as a fundamental factor in privatization. Foreign acquisitions can and should be considered by East European countries as a major network of highways, but it can by no means be envisaged as a 'fast lane' in the direction of a fully-fledged, Western-type market economy.

Privatization and state finances

Most East European governments want to sell state-owned properties rather than distribute them free of charge, in order to earn revenues from the sales. To get something in return for a valuable good is a general rule of exchange; thus, it is a reasonable demand of any seller to be reimbursed. However, does this general rule inevitably apply to East European privatization? Does privatization fall within the general category of exchange by all means? What are the specific arguments of East European governments that support their claims for reimbursement?

We discussed the peculiarities of so-called 'state ownership' in a command economy in Chapter 1. I showed that state ownership meant *de facto* property rights of a broadly defined *nomenklatura*. After the communist political system had been abolished and, at last, a democratically elected parliament had come to represent the people of a country in a genuine way – and the executive body of the parliament's majority, the government, was supposed to act in accordance with the will of the majority of the people – state ownership of a nation's property acquired a completely new meaning. In fact, state ownership itself represents an equitable share of property rights of all citizens of the state. Consequently, when state bureaucracies transfer the property rights of a state's assets, they do so as agents with limited authority of a country's citizens. Thus, they can sell the state-owned property to domestic or foreign private buyers, but the revenues earned from those sales are not theirs but belong to the country's citizens as a whole. (Agents are reimbursed in return for their services, but not as owners of the disposed-of properties.)[58] In principle, those revenues could be distributed directly among citizens first and carry taxes on the derived incomes later. However, in practice, such a solution would not be feasible because of the capacity constraints of central bureaucracies and because of the enormous costs such transfers would involve. Moreover, as long as a country's citizenry entrusts state institutions with the utilization of state-owned

58 A fully consistent solution would take into account the initial property share of a domestic private buyer in the state-owned properties: this is the essence of the Hungarian Tibor Liska's proposition. However, because of the lack of capital markets in an economy in transition, it is impossible to tell the real value of state-owned properties before those properties have actually been sold to their final private owners; consequently, the total value of state-owned assets that would be established beforehand could only be arbitrary. In addition, an attempt by a government to calculate the value of total assets and include those values in every single privatization deal would incur tremendous bureaucratic and transaction costs. Those costs would have to be charged on the people, and that would in turn reduce the net value of their properties.

property for the greatest possible benefit of all citizens, revenues earned from property sales can be channelled back to the economy in more efficient ways – and provide longer-term returns to citizens – than by distributing those revenues as personal incomes.

It follows from this argument that the free distribution of the state-owned property is also fully consistent with the transition from genuine state ownership to private ownership. To what extent, in what institutional arrangements and by what techniques free distribution can and should be pursued is a matter of serious economic concern and to some extent is related to politics. Thus, the evidence shows that free distribution schemes are not very popular among East European people, perhaps because they are unfamiliar with the practical details and consequences of free distribution. In addition, after 45 (in the former USSR 74) years of the communist governments' lack of credibility, and having gained mixed impressions concerning the new regimes' credibility, people are suspicious. They may suspect that some hidden costs or a concealed trap must be behind a government's 'generosity' when it intends to give them something free of charge. Nobody really dared to explain to people that the state-owned property belongs to them and state administrations do not own but merely administer the citizens' property.[59] Thus, the East European countries' 'absorption capacity' with respect to free distribution is fairly limited. In addition, the equivalent capacity of institutional owners is also constrained by the fact that any scheme of free distribution requires new institutions and considerable abilities on the part of the state bureaucracy in the initial phase of the process. In addition, there would be a need for a great number of managers with very special skills and expertise in the management of the potential funds or holdings in order to handle the assets behind the distributed property titles. Last but not least, different schemes of a free distribution might be an optimal way of transforming the property rights and transferring managerial obligations to special institutions in the case of certain groups of properties,

---

59 'The country is yours, you build it for yourself!' was a heavily publicized slogan of the communist parties after the Second World War. Nobody really believed it, but many 'interpreted' this slogan as a licence to physically take home a part of his factory or office, as his own property. Stealing state property on a large scale was and still is a common thing to do in East European countries. This fact certainly restrains government officials from publicizing the citizens' ownership rights too loudly.

but it might not be for others. I shall discuss these issues in detail in the next chapter.

What arguments do East European governments use to back their claim for state revenues from property sales? They point to the fact that during the past four decades East European states have accumulated a large internal debt, the amount of which matches the book value of state-owned assets. The accumulation of government debt had been largely connected – directly or indirectly – to investments that materialized in those enterprises and service monopolies which are now to be privatized. Consequently, governments consider state-owned assets as securities for internal debts. In addition to, and to some extent in close connection with, the accumulation of an internal debt, most East European countries carry a substantial external debt (in convertible currencies). For instance, in Hungary the amount of the gross external debt is nearly equal to the book value of state-owned enterprises, but it equals the amount of the internal government debt as well. Thus, state-owned property is regarded as an asset against both internal and external liabilities. The Hungarian government has asserted on several occasions that it intends to use revenues obtained from property sales for reducing the country's internal and external debt.

The assumption that the internal and external debt and the accumulation of state-owned assets are interrelated in a circular way in the East European countries cannot be considered totally false. Links among the three factors do exist, but no single one of them can explain exclusively any of the other two. (To give but one example: the amount of the Hungarian external debt may and did change considerably because of the shifts in interest rates and exchange rates of convertible currencies; however, changes in the interest rates on the international financial markets bore no relation whatsoever to the value of domestic fixed assets.) The striking similarity of the magnitude of the internal and external debt and the book value of state-owned assets is a 'cosmic connection' rather than an equation that could be related to the three variables mentioned above. Moreover, even if a static equation among the different debts and property values could be established, that would not imply a unique solution either for debt management or for the privatization of state-owned enterprises.

Obviously, a country's external debt can be reduced by using hard currency revenues from property sales for the repayment of the debt, but it ought not to be done under any circumstances. After all, it is not a reduction of the debt, but rather the financing of the outstanding debt obligations, that is required from a country that intends to obey the conventional rules of international financial markets. And financing the debt can be accomplished in many different ways (for example, by taking out fresh loans, or by achieving an increasing export surplus on the foreign trade balance, or by attracting a growing amount of foreign direct investment).

As was outlined above, it is not the total amount of the internal debt that must concern a government the most, but rather the current deficit of the state budget and its financing. The state budget deficit is connected with state-owned enterprises to the extent that governments are willing to spend budget revenues on subsidizing loss-making enterprises. (The direct and indirect interrelations between the state budget and the state-owned enterprises are more complex than suggested here, but for the sake of simplicity I neglect the other aspects.) On the other hand, revenues from property sales might be used by governments to reduce the amount of internal debt, but this would not necessarily result in a reduction, let alone elimination, of the state budget deficit. (A part of the deficit may be erased, to the extent that government revenues from privatization are used for a reduction of the government's debt to the central bank, since even today East European governments do not borrow on the money markets at a market rate of interest in order to finance their budget deficit, but they 'borrow' from the central bank instead, at a much lower interest rate than the actual market would ordain or at a realistic rate of interest. A part of the difference between the interest rate paid by the government to the central bank and a realistic market rate shows up in the state budget as an expenditure item.)

However, would revenues from privatization serve the East European countries' interests in the most efficient way possible, if those revenues had been used by governments for debt reduction? Or, would it not be more helpful to the private economy and more useful to the society at large if those revenues were channelled back directly to the private sector or to the crumbling infrastructure (or, indeed, to both)? Infrastructure needs to be upgraded in any case and by all possible means, in order to make it capable of supporting the private sector's development and to integrate services in a market economy. Considering all the factors outlined above, there are substantial grounds for doubt that East European governments would follow the most efficient direction of privatization if they regarded state finances as a decisive factor in determining how to privatize properties and how to use revenues from property sales. That such doubts are well founded can be supported by the fact that the Hungarian government, for instance, decided in October 1991 to use a substantial share of revenues from privatization for covering a part of the state budget deficit forecast for 1992. The government planned to use about HUF 20 bn ($260 million) for this purpose, that is, an amount equivalent to the total state income from privatization between June 1990 and June 1991. Ultimately, the government spent about HUF 36 bn on financing the state budget deficit from the SPA's revenues from property sales. Thus, the Hungarian government 'invented' a way of wasting the country's resources twice: first, when they were invested in state-owned enterprises, and now by financing the government's economic policy – especially fiscal policy – that has so far resulted in a modest pay-off.

The conflict persists between the East European governments' short-term interest in maintaining or restoring fiscal balance – and, in addition, servicing the countries' outstanding debt – and the longer-term tasks of supporting private investors who would be willing to restructure the ailing industries. The short-term pressures are felt much more strongly by the governments than the longer-term tensions – such as chronic unemployment and an continuing economic recession – that result from the slow pace of privatization and restructuring. Consequently, a vicious circle may develop in the East European countries: the governments need to attract a perpetually increasing inflow of money from foreign investors to service the debt, and more and more private savings to finance the deficit in the state budget. The satisfaction of these needs requires the interest rates on money deposits to be high enough to compensate for the risk faced by foreign or domestic private investors. However, the higher the real rate of interest – and the more attractive for foreign investors to keep their investment in bank accounts – the smaller the domestic or foreign enterpreneurs' propensity to invest in companies. Thus, the government's priority for a short-term fiscal balance may drastically reduce the amount of domestic and foreign private investment capital available for privatization and restructuring.

Privatization and restructuring

Although the settlement of private property rights and the comprehensive privatization of state-owned property are the most important preconditions for, as well as organic components of, the economic transition in Eastern Europe, these factors cannot automatically ensure a fully-fledged economic transformation. Another unavoidable task that East European countries face is a profound restructuring of their economies. If privatization is considered to be an extremely complex and difficult process, restructuring can be regarded as an even more challenging one. Ostensibly, sorting out the issues of private property rights and the subsequent privatization of a substantial part of the state-owned assets can be accomplished within a relatively short period (although it now seems as though privatization is actually progressing much more slowly in Eastern Europe than would be feasible and desirable). By contrast, it is realistic to consider that the 'physical' restructuring of the decrepit industries, along with the creation of financial institutions and capital markets and the reintegration of East European countries into the world economy, and, in addition, overcoming the social tensions that arise from rapidly growing unemployment, will take a decade at least. Therefore, if nothing else, the difference between privatization and restructuring, simply as regards their different time-span, would suggest that it is reasonable to make an analytical – and also policy – distinction between the two.

The privatization programmes of the East European governments do not indicate a clear distinction between privatization and restructuring. One gains the impression that East European governments are embroiled in controversy in this regard. On the one hand, it seems that governments have blindly placed their faith in privatization to take care of the complete restructuring of formerly state-owned property after privatization. Governments do not even attempt to assess different methods of privatization from the perspective of whether a specific way of turning properties over to private hands does or does not have any impact on the future utilization of those properties. On the other hand, state agencies, especially branch ministries, put a considerable effort into elaborating 'structural policy programmes' for different industries and individual companies. The chief argument of ministries for doing this is usually that a substantial part of the assets will remain state-owned for a considerable period of time. This will occur – as government officials argue – either because attractive offers from private investors for the purchase of individual enterprises do not exist, or because ministries want to retain specific enterprises in state hands as so-called 'strategic companies', and perhaps let them be privatized later, after a thorough upgrading. ('Upgrading' is meant, on most occasions, to signify an effort to boost the sale price of an enterprise.)

While in certain privatization cases the East European governments' expectations may be well founded as regards the impact of privatization on restructuring, in others they may not be. An example for the former case might be 'small-scale' privatization when the new private owner of a retail shop or restaurant would, in all probability, refurbish, redecorate and properly advertise her or his business. Another case would be when a substantial industrial investor (a so-called 'core investor')[60] is willing to acquire a substantial share of an East European enterprise and inject additional capital into it. As far as governmental structural policies and the restructuring of enterprises commanded by state bureaucracies are concerned, the wisdom of the command economy – whose legacy it is intended should be abandoned by the new East European regimes, supposedly as fast as possible – as well as most of the evidence of the advanced industrialized countries shows that a profound and rational restructuring of a complex economy cannot be achieved by central bureaucracies. There is no doubt that governments can foster the restructuring efforts of companies and make those changes less painful by several market-compatible devices, such as preferential loans, tax and tariff policies. In addition, governments and parliaments can design privatization programmes and institutions that are favourable for, rather than detrimental to, the enterprises' and industries' restructuring. But governments cannot – nor must they – restructure enterprises by acting as 'dispatchers' or managers.

Restructuring of the East European economies entails numerous

60 The term was used by Lipton and Sachs (1990), p.317.

changes that must proceed, if not hand in hand, at least in a consistent manner, taking into account the most important impacts of any one aspect of restructuring upon the others. Thus, governments and other central state agencies do have a coordinatory role of a special kind: they must clearly define the legal and economic constraints placed upon the radical changes and they must design instruments to cushion the most severe social burdens of the transition. Beyond this 'negative' regulatory role, however, governments should refrain from coordinating different processes of the restructuring. Restructuring must include, among other things, a 'physical' reshaping of individual enterprises and whole industries, and a profound alteration to the organizational, and especially management, structure of companies. In addition, restructuring must be accompanied by a shift of the current statistical and accounting system of companies to the standard procedures of the market economies, by the creation of private financial and capital market institutions and regulatory bodies for those markets, and by an ensuing rearrangement of the structure of employment and the labour market.[61] This complex process of micro- and mezo-level changes will, in all certainty, result in a radical shift of the East European economies' branch structure, as it will produce a size structure of companies completely different from the current one. In particular, the share of several sectors, such as agriculture, mining and traditional branches of heavy industry – industries that have been 'overweight' in these countries – will diminish as a result of the restructuring. In addition, most of the large state-owned enterprises and combines that had been assembled administratively will be replaced by a large number of medium and small private companies.

It is impossible even to list all the tasks and problems that must be tackled by private owners and governments during the restructuring process: suffice it to mention only a few of these. A major difficulty facing East European industrial enterprises is that most of them delivered the bulk of their products to the CMEA markets. These markets have collapsed and East European state-owned enterprises are left in the swamp of a disintegrating autarkic economic community. It is important to note that it was not simply the enterprises' production lines, equipment and products that had been designed especially for

---

61 The reform of the East European accounting systems is discussed in OECD (1991).

the needs of the CMEA markets: rather the whole internal structure of enterprise management and operation, and also the enterprises' ways and means of establishing foreign contacts (that is, factors determining how to do business and with whom) were intended to satisfy the requirements of East European trade, but are hardly adaptable to Western markets.

Among East European enterprises, companies of the defence industry are hit twice over by the collapse of East European trade. In additition to the overall problems of losing markets, these enterprises must either close down or introduce products completely different from the present ones, and they must instal new technologies. Enterprises of the traditional heavy industries, such as metallurgy, shipbuilding and heavy machinery, can hardly avoid enormous cuts in production and employment, or even total closures.

In discussions about East European restructuring, agriculture is only rarely mentioned. An obvious reason for this neglect may be that most East European countries have suffered from a frequently recurring shortage of food and other agricultural products (the only exception has been Hungary since the late 1960s), whereas 'restructuring' is meant to eliminate surplus and redundant assets, beginning with employment and production, and create new capacity later. However, agriculture, too, is bloated in all East European countries. The vast resources that were poured into that sector have been used in an extremely wasteful manner. For instance, in the USSR, agriculture has taken up 17–23 per cent of the country's gross investments since Khrushchev's time.[62] No other single branch of the Soviet economy was granted such a share of investment resources during the past three and a half decades, with the exception of defence. In Hungary, the '*Wunderkind*' of Eastern Europe as regards agriculture, successes were mostly due to large-scale grain and meat production for the Soviet market. However, costs did not count! Now as the Russian and other CIS markets are shrinking and Hungarian producers are not being bailed out by the government, a large majority of agricultural cooperatives are going bankrupt. Hectic swings between over-production and subsequent severe shortages (for example, a shortage of pigmeat during the summer of 1991) signal the

62 *Narodnoe khozyaistvo SSSR*, various issues.

agricultural crisis in Hungary. Consequently, the restructuring of agriculture is becoming an urgent task in all East European countries if widespread shortages of basic food items are to be avoided. (In agriculture, a sensible programme of privatization can contribute to a relatively fast and efficient restructuring much more easily than in many industrial branches.)

Last but not least, public infrastructure and services in general need comprehensive restructuring and upgrading, as fast as is practicable. Telecommunications, transportation and financial services especially must be enhanced in capacity and upgraded in both technological and management terms.[63] A considerable development of services in Eastern Europe is important not only from the perspective that a sound market economy cannot emerge without those services: it is also important because new services can provide some of the unemployed with jobs and increase the standard of living of the population by improving the quality of life in an era when real wages are likely to fall for most citizens.

In addition to East European studies and programmes, there exists a fairly large number of works by Western economists on the subject of East European restructuring. The best-known are those by Lipton and Sachs and by Blanchard *et al.*[64] Lipton and Sachs address only the issues of restructuring as that concerns large state-owned enterprises. They put forward the proposition that restructuring should be incorporated into the process of privatization, recommending a scheme of free distribution of the large enterprises' assets that would include an allotment of a share of properties to 'core investors'.[65] It is not fully clear from Lipton and Sachs's description whether core investors – presumably foreign – should pay for their share and if so, how sales prices should be decided by the sellers. We may assume that the authors would recommend a genuine sale rather than a handing over of the state-owned property to foreign investors free of charge. But then a serious problem would resurface: the sales value of assets must be determined somehow – one of the most contro- versial issues Lipton and Sachs most wanted to avoid. Assuming rather than

63 I discussed the issues of public infrastructure and services during transition in Major (1991d).
64 Lipton and Sachs (1990), and Blanchard *et al.* (1991).
65 Lipton and Sachs (1990), pp.313-20.

proving that the issue of asset evaluation can be resolved, Lipton and Sachs envisage a restructuring within the framework of mutual funds that would exercise the property rights and the rights and responsibilities of management of the large enterprises allocated to them. Mutual funds with core investors among their co-owners and executives should act as 'restructurers' of the enterprises at least in the initial phase of ownership transformation.

Without denying the merits of Lipton and Sachs's privatization plan, doubts may be raised about the efficiency and soundness of their scheme when it comes to restructuring. Institutional owners can be very efficient in reallocating capital from less to more lucrative businesses that already exist. However, it is unrealistic to expect that mutual funds and other institutional owners, with or without core investors, will 'physically' restructure individual enterprises or create new production and service facilities in large numbers that can later become targets of their capital-rechannelling endeavours. Institutional owners may be able to oversee the profound restructuring of a few companies, but not several hundred, let alone thousands, of them. Obviously, institutional owners may assign the task of restructuring of different enterprises to different groups of managers. However, managerial and organizational skills are very scarce resources in Eastern Europe. In addition, most of the enterprises need a more or less individual approach to their restructuring. Consequently, institutional owners would encounter tremendous difficulties in finding a sufficient number of skilful managers able to cope with the very complex issues of reshaping hundreds of companies. On the other hand, concentrating managers and managerial skills in huge institutions would reduce rather than increase the managers' efficiency, since managers must become integrated into the bureaucracy of an institutional owner in addition to managing company affairs.

Arguing in favour of their privatization scheme with free distribution, Lipton and Sachs stress that '... most enterprises should be privatized in a common manner, to avoid debates between the government and individual enterprises.'[66] It is not fully clear from their study just how far 'a common manner' of privatization should be extended. Should a 'common manner' be applied to the restructuring of enterprises, too? The authors do not openly suggest

66 Ibid., pp.322-3.

this solution, but their line of reasoning allows for such an interpretation. However, it would be disastrous for the East European economies if all or even just most enterprises were restructured in a uniform manner, by applying some pre-determined criteria – made up by the bureaucracies of institutional owners – and without looking carefully into the different aspects of an enterprise's organization, management, staff, market conditions and prospects. Of course, there are a number of general criteria that any company should meet if it aims to survive without government support. Specifically, a company must produce positive profits, it must be run efficiently, it must have the intellectual capacity to innovate, and it must be flexible enough to readjust if needed.

Corporate governance of companies is a common practice in advanced market economies and it is also feasible in Eastern Europe to a certain extent. However, corporate governance is a very sophisticated way of operation in the West – perhaps one of the most sophisticated ways – which has no real roots in Eastern Europe yet. At the same time, a certain remote resemblance between corporate governance and central planning poses the danger that East European governments would be tempted to resort to the traditional devices of the command economy as if those devices were 'almost the same' as their Western counterparts. Such a danger is far from hypothetical. Thus, for instance, the Hungarian government plans to set up state holding companies to act as 'mutual funds' of the state-owned assets and as agents of corporate governance, and, in June 1992, the Hungarian parliament adopted an 'Act on the Permanently State-Owned Property' that created a huge state holding company for managing about 30–40 per cent of all state-owned assets on a long-term basis.[67]

There is a mass of evidence that leading politicians and government figures are willing to apply the very same measures and methods to regulate the economy as had been used by the old regime. The new regimes do so in the conviction – or at least the pretence – that 'we will apply those devices better because we are not communists'. We may conclude that corporate governance may be a way of privatizing and restructuring a limited number of state-owned enterprises, but it cannot be a part of an 'overall privatization package'. Realistically, an extensive network of corporate governance (a large number of huge

67 *Figyelő*, 2 July 1992.

private corporations) may be the result rather than a starting point of privatization and restructuring in Eastern Europe. (I shall return to this issue in the next chapter.)

Blanchard *et al.* outline a different approach to restructuring from that discussed above.[68] While, like Lipton and Sachs, they also are in favour of a free distribution of the state-owned property, Blanchard and his collaborators try to address privatization and restructuring as completely separate issues. I can fully agree with their intention as long as they make a clear distinction between these two aspects of East European economic transformation. I agree with them despite the fact that, in reality, privatization and restructuring cannot be fully disentangled. But it is important to keep them separate for purposes of discussion. I also accept their line of reasoning when they address the tasks of East European governments in restructuring (as mostly the tasks of a 'negative regulator' and general promoter). However, they seem to go rather too far in entrusting East European governments with actual involvement in individual cases of restructuring. On the other hand, the authors present an extremely radical view of how the restructuring of industries and individual enterprises – indeed, the restructuring of the economy as a whole – should take place.

To simplify their proposal somewhat, Blanchard *et al.* would 'erase' the bulk of the existing East European industries. According to them, real economic growth and investment can and should be expected only from the new private businesses, almost independent of the enterprises that are currently owned by the state.[69] The authors support their arguments by using scattered statistical data and they refer to the fact that 'The assessment of foreign technical experts who have examined a number of Polish firms is also very guarded'.[70] There is no doubt that most of the problems Blanchard and his colleagues mention concerning East European industries are relevant. Thus, production lines, technologies and organizational structures of most enterprises are obsolete; the legacy of CMEA trade is a great burden on the companies; moreover, Western investors who are willing to acquire East European properties usually say that it would

68 Blanchard *et al.* (1991), pp.59–94.
69 Although less straightforward, Kornai (1990) envisages a similar process of the state sector dying and the private sector gaining strength.
70 Blanchard *et al.* (1991), p.67.

be much easier for them to bulldoze those enterprises and start investment from scratch rather than bother with reshaping existing factories. This argument is frequently raised especially in the case of the former GDR: Western analysts argue that the *Treuhandanstalt* cannot proceed faster because most East German companies have negative market values, hence West German investors are unwilling to buy East German assets. And if this is the case for the former GDR – a country that was considered the most advanced in Eastern Europe – the position cannot be better for any other East European country. However, what analysts fail to recognize is the fact that the negative values of the East German enterprises are due basically to two factors: first, the monetary union of the two Germanies increased the price of East German labour to an extreme extent which, in turn, pushed almost all companies into bankruptcy; secondly, such respected intelligence agencies as the CIA and other prominent Western research institutes estimated the East German productivity as 80 per cent (!) of the West German level, so when West German investors finally faced actual productivity of East German industry of 20 per cent of the West German level at best, their expectations were completely demolished. This fact also largely contributed to the West German investors' unwillingness to acquire East German properties. Still, a negative assessment may be justified for several East European enterprises, although a more careful consideration would still be appropriate.

Before bulldozing Eastern Europe, some facts should be considered. First, East European companies, both private and state-owned, already accomplished a remarkable switch of exports from the CMEA markets to Western markets in Hungary and Poland in 1990, and sustained this during 1991. The shift in Hungarian and Polish exports occurred after the transferable rouble had been replaced by convertible currencies as the only accepted means of payment on 1 January 1991 in all East European countries. A similar change is occurring in Eastern Germany and in the ČSFR, although at a slower pace than in the other three countries mentioned above. One may correctly argue that a considerable part of these exports was inefficient, that is, deliveries were made at a price below production costs. In addition, growing exports to the market economies were accompanied by even more rapidly increasing imports from those countries. These are worrying facts that point to the need for a more sensible economic policy on the part of the East European governments and for a more rapid transformation of state-owned enterprises into private companies. At the same time, these facts do not support a 'bulldozer policy' of restructuring in Eastern Europe.

Secondly, and not independently of what has been written above, East European enterprises might be unable to produce sophisticated, high-technology products on a large scale, but many of them can manufacture low or medium-level products to Western standards. Or rather, they will be able to do so after privatization and some restructuring that does not require a vast amount of capital and human skills. This might not be a sensible strategy for all enterprises (since it is highly desirable that completely new products, among them high-technology goods, should be produced in the greatest possible number), but it can be a reasonable option for several of them, at least for an interim period. The greatest efforts are needed in the short run in the packaging and marketing of East European products. An inhabitant of Washington may want to do her or his everyday shopping in a Safeway supermarket, just as a citizen of Stockholm may prefer to buy her or his couture at NK or in elegant boutiques. Yet many Washingtonians shop at Magruder's (an inexpensive and not particularly elegant, 'down-market' grocery store) and look for less expensive products, just as many Stockholmers dress from Hennes & Mauritz or from even less expensive and less famous stores. Thus, there may be a niche for many East European products even on Western markets if those products are properly presented in Western countries.

To 'descend' to lower quality markets or to markets for less sophisticated products may be at least as much a problem of East European pride as one of demand. For instance, all East European countries have built up a sizeable electronics industry that cannot withstand Western competition at the level of end-products, software and high-technology components. But sections of the very same companies would be suitable candidates – although not in their current size, of course – for producing components, spare parts and less technology-intensive products for Western companies. And the new companies could catch up with software and high-technology production gradually. However, this idea sounds like an insult to many 'captains of industry' in the flagships of East European industrial enterprises.

Finally, I showed in Chapter 2 that the bulk of the East European state-owned assets comprises real estate and factory buildings, and the machinery and equipment, worth little more than scrap, account for less than 30 per cent of the assets. Of course, most of these buildings need considerable improvement, but not all of them are entirely worthless. This fact should not be disregarded when the restructuring of the East European economies is under discussion. This is not to say, by any means, that restructuring can proceed without closing down a large number of enterprises or their parts, at least, nor do I consider East European real estate as 'life savers' of the crumbling economies. My only point was that a unified solution for the economic restructuring of the East European countries might do more harm than good to the prospects for a successful transition to a market economy.

5.3 THE INITIAL RESULTS OF EAST EUROPEAN PRIVATIZATIONS

While East European programmes and Western concepts of privatization deserved a fairly lengthy discussion, our account of the actual accomplishments in privatization to date can be rather brief. The main reason for this is that privatization has yielded modest results so far. A few qualifying comments on the word 'modest' are in order. As we shall see below, several thousand joint ventures between domestic and Western companies have been established in each East European country during the past two years, 1991–92, and foreign capital has started flowing into the banking sector as well. In addition, thousands of small state-owned companies in retail trade, catering and other services have been turned over to private hands and an even larger number of new small private companies have been set up. Moreover, several dozen and in some countries even hundreds of medium-sized and large state-owned enterprises have been privatized, at least partially. How can these results be regarded as modest? If we compare the numbers and relative asset values of privatization with those of Great Britain, France or any other country with a market economy that are regarded as having been the forerunners of privatization in the West (and South), East European countries have done considerably more on this count than most of their Western counterparts.

However, if we set the East European results in privatization against the needs of a successful economic transformation, and against the feasible speed and scope of privatization that could have been achieved in the last two years, then we find the accomplishments much less impressive, indeed largely inadequate. Even if we disregard the fact that the 'true' number of privatizations – as reported by the East European official statistics – leaves a considerable degree of confusion and uncertainty in the mind of the observer (since it is not always clear if an enterprise that was reported as privatized had been in fact turned over to private hands, or only a minority share of the company had been sold to private owners and the majority share remained in state hands), there is still little ground for satisfaction. What is even more dissatisfying than the amount of privatization is the confusion about the privatization programmes and institutions and their inconsistent nature. Privatization in Eastern Europe cannot be considered a task that can be fulfilled in the same way as central plans were in the command economy. Privatization should, first of all, mean the creation of a comprehensive network of private ownership institutions that can serve as a solid ground for the emergence of individual private owners and a sound market economy. This is precisely the process that is not proceeding swiftly and in a satisfactory manner in the East European countries. East European governments are bound to regard privatization as a matter of fulfilling quantitative plans rather than bothering with institution building. Instead, governments try to use each individual privatization case for boosting their short-term political goals instead.

Before turning to the general issues of institution building for private ownership, let me first discuss the actual results of the East European privatizations as these are perceived by the governments and by outside observers. Marvin Jackson and Paul Hare and Irena Grosfeld have provided us with a fairly detailed assessment of privatization in Eastern Europe.[71] In 1992, Jozef van Brabant, Bruno Dallago, and a team of the Central European University headed by

---

71 Jackson (1990) and (1991), and Hare and Grosfeld (1991).

Roman Frydman, Andrzej Rapaczynski and John S. Earle produced longer studies of the East European privatization process.[72] Of course, a considerable amount of information could be added to Jackson's, Hare and Grosfeld's, van Brabant's or Dallago's studies, or to the reports of the Central European University, if one wished to dig down to the specific issues of individual privatization cases. Such an analysis would be worthwhile, but it is beyond the scope of this study. On the following pages I shall assess the results of East European privatizations only for the larger, more or less homogeneous groups of properties that were described in Chapters 3 and 4.

I suggested above that East European governments consider foreign direct investment and joint ventures with foreign participants as the main course of privatization. Let us begin our assessment with this group. Foreign direct investment started flowing into Eastern Europe in significant quantities only in the late 1980s. The amount of foreign capital invested in the East European countries each year remained well below one billion dollars until 1989; then in 1990, the total value of direct foreign investment slightly exceeded that sum. Of this amount, Hungary took about 50 per cent, and the other half of the investment was shared by the other East European countries (Poland ranked second among them with about $300 million). In 1991, the total amount of foreign investments exceeded $3 bn, of which Hungary retained its absolute majority share, with an invested amount of $1.5 bn (about half of all foreign investments in Eastern Europe). However, we must add that from this amount only about $770 million was equity capital and contributions in kind by foreign investors: the rest was deposited by foreigners in Hungarian banks. The ČSFR was catching up fast, with a few but sizeable joint ventures that have been or were planned to be set up with a considerable foreign participation (Volkswagen, Siemens and ABB are heavy investors in that country);[73] by the end of 1991, about 4,900 joint ventures were operating there. In Poland, the amount of foreign investment was expected to increase substantially (by about $500-600 million) too, in 1991 (see Table 5.1 below).

In the first half of 1992, the picture concerning foreign direct investment was mixed. The growth rate of such investment in the East

72 See UN ECE (1992), Dallago (1992), and Frydman *et al.* (1993a, 1993b).
73 See *RFE Report on Eastern Europe*, 22 November 1991, pp.6-12.

Table 5.1 Joint ventures in Eastern Europe up to 1990, and 1991

	Number of joint ventures		Capital invested (mn $)		Foreign capital per joint venture, 1,000 $	
	1990	*1991*	*1990*	*1991*	*1990*	*1991*
ČSFR	178	2,937c	131	172c	734	59c
Germany	n.a	200d	n.a	..	..	..
Hungary	5,250	8,250a	1,450	1,950a	276	236a
Polandb	2,507	3,740a	351	580a	140	155a
USSRe	2,905	<3,000a	-250	-800a	87	267a
USSRf	2,050	n.a	3,152	n.a	1,537	n.a

[a] until 30 June 1991; [b] joint ventures and companies owned fully by foreigners (invested capital includes cash, apports and credits (!) borrowed by foreigners); [c] until 23 July 1991; [d] until 31 August 1991 (the total number of companies sold either to West Germans or foreigners was 3,000); [e] Soviet official data; [f] UN ECE data (US $1=0.63 Rouble).

Sources: WIIW *Mitgliedinformation*, No.8, 1991, p.28; *Tydenik Hospodarskych Novin*, No.38, 19 September 1991; Schrettl (1991); *MTI Econews*, 23 September 1991; *Maly Rocznik Statystyczny 1991*, p.279; *Rzeczpospolita*, No.8 (29); *Gazeta Bankowa*, 14 September 1991, *SSSR v tsifrakh v 1990 godu*, Goskomstat SSSR, Moscow, 1991, p.72; *Ekonomika i zhizn'*, No.30, July 1991; *East West Joint Ventures News*, UN ECE, No.7, February 1991, p.16.

European countries – apart from large West German investment in eastern Germany – began to decelerate. The CSFR managed to attract larger amounts – the total value of foreign direct investment increased to $2 bn in that country, with another $3 bn under discussion[74] – and Hungary's prospects for the same year also seemed reasonable, with receipts of about $1 bn in the first half of the year. In Poland, Romania and the republics of the former USSR, however, political instability scared foreign investors away from taking substantial risk, and with the disintegration of the CSFR, the positive trends may be reversed there, too.

The largest foreign investors in Eastern Europe are the USA, Western Germany and Austria. The next group consists of Canada,

74 *Financial Times,*, 3 July 1992.

Switzerland, Italy and Sweden. Japan has taken a more cautious stand than the other countries so far, but it has also started some important projects, in Hungary for example. The composition of foreign investments, as regards the size and branch affiliation of the investor companies, is striking. On the one hand, some of the very largest Western multinationals, such as, for instance, General Motors, AT&T, General Electric, Westinghouse, Boeing, McDonell Douglas, Siemens, Volkswagen, Ericsson, ABB, Tetrapak and some of the leading Western banks have entered joint ventures with East European partners (this list is far from exhaustive.) And on the other hand, thousands of the smallest Western companies, frequently just individual businessmen, have created joint ventures with East European companies. The vast majority of the joint ventures operate in the service sector – especially retail trading – but the very largest ones are becoming important players in high-technology industries (such as car and vehicle production, electronics and telecommunication equipment, aircraft maintenance, and so forth).

Since mid-to-late 1991 the number of joint ventures has further increased, as has the amount of foreign capital invested in the East European countries. For instance, in Hungary the number of joint ventures amounted to about 13,000 by September 1992 and the foreign capital invested added up to $3.5 bn. By the end of the year, foreign direct investment – in kind and in cash deposited in Hungarian banks – added up to $4.2 bn. In early 1992, the inflow of foreign capital also increased in the ČSFR and Russia, while it decelerated in Poland, and remained very low in the other East European countries. But even in countries with sizeable foreign direct investment, the impact of joint ventures on the economies still remained almost negligible.

The literature on the legal and economic conditions, experiences, barriers to and successes of East European joint ventures is immense. I do not intend to discuss these aspects from a micro-perspective, but rather I shall mention a few issues that have an overall impact on joint ventures in general. As is shown in Table 5.1, the current number and the rate of expansion of joint ventures are impressive in some East European countries.[75] However, the amount and share of

75 According to the latest Hungarian reports, almost 10,000 joint ventures existed in that country at the end of September 1991, to the tune of $1.7 bn foreign participation: see *MTI Econews*, 5 December 1991.

the foreign capital invested so far is well below the level of, say, foreign investments in the South European, Southeast Asian or even South American countries, let alone the level that East European governments hoped for (see Table 5.2).

Table 5.2   The share of foreign capital in the total fixed assets of the East European countries in 1991 (in per cent)

ČSFR	East Germany	Hungary	Poland	USSR
0.2	20.0*	3.5	0.6	0.4

* including West German investments.

Sources: As in Tables 2.1–2.5, Table 3.1; *Tydenik Hospodarskych Novin*, No.38, 19 September 1991; *Magyar Hírlap*, 13 November 1991.

As was mentioned above, the amount and share of foreign capital further increased in most East European countries. In Hungary, the amount of foreign capital invested relative to the total value of national assets increased to 4 per cent by mid-1992. Similarly in the ČSFR or in the Russian Federation the share of foreign capital increased, too, but it was still unable to exert a dominant influence on those countries' economic development.

East European governments have tried to attract foreign companies by offering generous tax privileges to foreign investors, and, besides tax concessions, government officials use personal persuasion all the time on their meetings with representatives of Western governments and business communities. However, while tax concessions to Western investors may 'sweeten' the joint venture deals, those concessions alone cannot trigger a massive capital inflow to Eastern Europe. Tax holidays rather provided an opportunity for legalized tax evasion by domestic companies, and they served as a gift to Western businessmen who wanted to make a quick profit. Serious investors have been much more interested in the legal rules of profit and capital transfers, in the state of local infrastructures (above all in telecommunication and transport), regulations on banking activities and the stability and level of convertibility of the local currency, in a transparent and sensible system of property rights and in the level of liberalization of enterprise activities in general.

On several occasions, a debt-for-equity swap or a debt-for-environmental protection swap on a substantial scale was proposed by East European governments and Western economists, too, especially in the cases of Poland, Hungary and the former USSR. But, however attractive and original these proposals may sound, they remained illusions instead of becoming reality in Eastern Europe. Western governments and companies may be blamed for being short-sighted or selfish in not showing more interest in these proposals. However, nobody has yet really addressed the enormous practical difficulties of putting such ideas into practice. The fact is that East European countries owe their debt to Western governments and banks; consequently, a debt-for-equity swap, in other words, channelling East European assets into Western companies, would require central coordination on an immense scale among Western banks, companies and governments. But the necessary devices for such central coordination simply do not exist in a market economy, and in all likelihood they would not be tolerated by Western private businesses if a government tried to create such a mechanism.

In conclusion, it is realistic to say that foreign direct investment has not become a factor, and it is most unlikely that it will ever become one, such as would eliminate the pain for East European governments, companies and entrepreneurs in laying the foundations of private ownership and a market economy. Moreover, it is equally unrealistic to expect that privately-owned foreign capital will account for 25–30 per cent of an East European country's total assets,[76] if the basic institutions of a market economy with dominant private ownership have not emerged or been created beforehand. However, if privatization should indeed engulf an East European economy, there is every reason to predict a massive inflow of foreign direct investment in the medium term.

Another area that has been characterized by successes rather than by failures in Eastern Europe is small-scale privatization ('small privatization' is the term used in the ČSFR and Poland, while it is

---

76 A Hungarian state secretary forecast the share of foreign capital in Hungary by 1993-94: see *Magyar Hírlap*, 13 November 1991.

called 'pre-privatization' in Hungary). The thousands of retail stores, even chain stores, restaurants, networks of household appliance maintenance and repair businesses and other types of small services have been leased out or auctioned off to private entrepreneurs from Albania to Poland. For instance, in the ČSFR some 10,000 out of 19,347 small companies that were included in the small privatization programme have already been turned over to private hands, and the average actual sale price of these small companies exceeded the average initial bidding price by 50 per cent.[77] Auctioning off the small companies was left completely to the local government authorities – in other words, the process was extensively decentralized, a fact that to a large extent contributed to its success. In Poland, small privatization also progressed with remarkable speed: in towns, 90 per cent of retail trade companies and restaurants have been privatized, and by early 1991 the number of small private establishments and individual entrepreneurs already exceeded 1.2 million;[78] since then, this number has increased still further.[79] Even in Albania, auctioning off – often simply giving away – small businesses is progressing at a rapid pace.[80] The process may accelerate soon in the republics of the disintegrating USSR, too.

In Hungary, although small private businesses have mushroomed since as early as the mid-1980s, the new government's small privatization plan is proceeding more slowly than in the other East European countries. The programme started with almost 14,000 companies, but then this number was reduced to 10,000. A very complex and complicated legal act had been elaborated by the Hungarian government and endorsed by parliament in September 1990;[81] since then one thousand or so out of the 10,000 companies were auctioned off by the SPA, against 3,500 privatizations that had been planned for 1991. However, the process accelerated in 1992, and by the end of the year another 4,000 companies and shops were due to be privatized. According to figures of August 1992, this goal was

77 *Világgazdaság*, 9 November 1991, and *Privatization Newsletter of Czechoslovakia*, No.1, October 1991.
78 Mroz (1991), p.679.
79 See 'Privatization in Poland. Program and Achievements', op. cit.
80 Åslund and Sjöberg (1991).
81 I discussed this act and its consequences in Major (1991b).

proving realistic: about 3,000 small units had been auctioned off to private investors.[82]

The process of auctioning off companies was hindered by several factors. First, it was over-centralized, since each auction was organized and each initial bidding price was set by the SPA. Secondly, the initial sales price set by the SPA proved to be too high on several occasions. Consequently, 40 per cent of the organized auctions were completely unsuccessful in 1991. Third, a large part of the small businesses that are now for sale had been leased out to private entrepreneurs a few years ago, and consequently, the rights of the lease-holder clash with the intentions of the SPA. In addition, property rights of the local governments and the state, as regards the real estate in or on which different small businesses operate, have not been properly sorted out, and in consequence attempts at privatization are blocked for months because of legal disputes among the different 'players'.[83]

All in all, however, small privatization has made real progress in each East European country. In several of them, the appearance of thousands of private businesses has made life, especially in larger cities, more colourful and more pleasant (but also more expensive). The assortment of consumer products is large; shortages have by and large been eliminated. The attractive shop-windows in the inner cities leave Western visitors with the impression that 'Life cannot be as bad as we are told by East Europeans. These people just love to complain.' Unfortunately, though, despite the impressive development of small business, East Europeans are right when they show less admiration for, and greater reservation about, the results of privatization so far.

Alongside small privatization, turning state-owned apartments over to private owners is gathering momentum as well in the East European countries. It is mostly the local governments that are made responsible for the process, selling apartments to the tenants at a discounted price. Privatization may proceed more easily in countries where most apartments are state-owned, at least in towns, than in countries such as Hungary, where the vast majority of the people built and own the apartment themselves. Paradoxically as it may seem at

82 *Figyelő*, 6 August 1992.
83 *Heti Világgazdaság*, 16 November 1991, pp.79-81.

first glance, many Hungarians consider it to be a major injustice if rented apartments can be bought for a much lower price now than was usually paid for private apartments in the past.[84] In my opinion, the problem of giving apartments to tenants for a low but realistic price is 'inflated'. Fair solutions, not excessively meticulous methods, must be found to turn over the housing stock – the bulk of which is crumbling – to responsible private owners. In addition, the emergence of a sound housing market should be fostered by all available means.

Privatization of agricultural land is becoming a much more controversial issue in Eastern Europe than the privatization of those properties mentioned above. A misplaced emphasis on the property rights of past rather than current owners and an extremely over-politicized approach to reprivatization have resulted in complete chaos in several East European countries as regards the privatization of property in land and real estate. For instance in Eastern Germany, about 1.5 million claims for confiscated properties have been lodged with the *Treuhandanstalt*, creating a 'legal jungle' in that country;[85] it may take ten to fifteen years before the property rights can be sorted out there. Reprivatization of agricultural land is envisaged in Bulgaria, the ČSFR, Romania and several republics of the USSR as well. In Albania, agricultural land is being distributed among peasants who actually work on and derive a living from a given piece of land. In Hungary, a fairly sophisticated law on compensation and partial reprivatization was adopted by the parliament in April 1991, and about 140,000 claims for confiscated properties had been submitted by Hungarians by the end of October 1991;[86] by mid-1992, the number of claims had increased to almost 200,000. Original owners whose agricultural land was confiscated can physically regain a part of their lost properties, and the rest will be compensated for by a 'compensation voucher', the value of which will be calculated using a regressive scale. These compensation vouchers may be used to buy shares in privatized companies or they may be converted into a life annuity for their owners. The total amount of compensation is estimated to add up to HUF 100 bn ($1.3 bn). The adoption of the

---

84 Even Kornai found this issue so important and sensitive that he discussed it extensively in his book: see Kornai (1990), p.81.
85 *Financial Times*, 12 November 1991.
86 *Világgazdaság*, 31 October 1991.

'Compensation Act' almost brought about the downfall of the Hungarian government and is still considered by the vast majority of the population as a serious mistake.

Finally, what have been the results of the 'large privatization' in Eastern Europe? First, it must be emphasized that a thorough and comprehensive statistical analysis of the privatization of large state-owned enterprises has not been performed in any of the East European countries. State agencies responsible for privatization publish data on company transformations from time to time, but those data are unreliable and not sufficiently qualified. For instance, we do not have a clear picture of whether the companies reported by the state agencies as having been privatized really have been turned over to private hands, or only a minority share of the enterprises' assets sold to foreign and domestic private buyers. (Evidence supports the latter assumption for the majority of so-called 'privatized' companies.) Secondly, since large privatizations are completely centralized in each East European country, it is in the governments' and their agencies' interest to give an exaggerated account of the actual progress of privatization. 'Triumphal reports' on the successes achieved are assembled by state bureaucracies along very similar lines to the 'victorious reports' on the fulfilment of central mandatory plans devised by their predecessors. Thus, should privatization continue as it has so far, we cannot expect a more realistic assessment even later, when East European statistical systems are reconstructed to meet the needs of a new regime.

Bearing in mind the pitfalls of statistics, but assessing large privatizations on the basis of official sources, the actual results of privatization are still fairly meagre in all countries. The most important point to note is that large privatization is concentrated in the hands of East European governments, since separate state agencies or ministries were given responsibility for executing the governments' plans for large privatization.

In the ČSFR only a few 'showcases' can be mentioned as examples of large privatization. In these cases, the process occurred by commercializing a large state-owned enterprise (such as Škoda) first and selling its assets, or a majority of them, to foreign buyers. The Czechoslovak government expected that the implementation of a voucher scheme would accelerate the process; however, the population's interest in obtaining vouchers was initially modest. In addition, ever wider disagreement about the soundness of the voucher scheme was surfacing among government members and political parties in parliament, as a consequence of which the starting date of the voucher programme was postponed by the government by three months. In 1992, the distribution of vouchers finally started and it proved an unexpected success: 8.5 million people bought vouchers in the Czech and the Slovak Republics and 436 private mutual funds were established to invest the vouchers in the securities of 1,500 enterprises; 72 per cent of those who had bought vouchers invested their shares in such mutual funds.[87] However, after the national elections in which separatist groups won victory in Slovakia, the future of the voucher system came into question again in that part of the country.

Eastern Germany – notably the *Treuhandanstalt* – went the farthest among the East European countries as regards the number of privatized companies. Up to September 1991, some 3,000 East German enterprises had been sold to mostly West German investors.[88] A peculiar feature of the first phase of East German privatizations was that the number of enterprises retained by the state increased in tandem with the number of privatized companies. What happened in practice was that the *Treuhandanstalt* split East German enterprises into several units and then sold half of them to private owners. If this strange method of privatization were to drag on, the share of privatized companies relative to the total number of East German enterprises would still grow, but it could never reach 50 per cent. (I present below a fairly simple mathematical analysis of the different ways of privatization: see appendix to this section, pp.127–30, where I discuss the East German method as a special case.)

In 1992, *Treuhand* accelerated the process and it succeeded in privatizing another 4,000 enterprises. A new act entitled the state agency to privatize even companies whose original owners had submitted their claims but who were unwilling to match the terms of the most favourable offer. In addition, the agency started an aggressive campaign to attract foreign investors. It believes that all East German enterprises will be privatized by 1994.

87 *Financial Times*, 3 July 1992.
88 Schrettl, op. cit.

In Hungary, the State Property Agency regularly reports the numbers and asset values of 'enterprise transformation' and 'cases of state property protection'. Thus, three main programmes of privatization have been launched by the SPA so far. The first one was made public in September 1990, the second in December 1990, and the third a few weeks later. The first package consisted of twenty state-owned enterprises, and only three of them had been partially privatized by November 1991. The other two programmes have barely started. The total number of enterprises to be privatized by the SPA directly is planned to reach 130 or 140. According to the SPA's accounts, 161 state-owned enterprises started their conversion into joint stock companies or limited liability companies between March 1990 and July 1991. Among these conversions, 52 cases were successfully concluded by July 1991. The total book value of assets affected by conversions was a mere 5 per cent of the country's state-owned industrial assets. However, only 24.3 per cent of the assets of the transformed companies were sold to private (foreign) buyers, and 70.5 per cent was retained by the SPA![89] (The 5.2 per cent unaccounted for relates to the property shares of local governments.) By the end of the year, the number of transformed enterprises stood at about 120.

In 1992 the Hungarian government expected large privatization to accelerate. The number of enterprises under corporatization increased to 901 by the end of April 1992, and 282 of these were already converted into joint stock companies. (The total asset value of the corporatized companies is about one-quarter of the total value of productive state-owned assets.) Eight per cent of the assets of the corporatized companies was sold to foreign investors, while 86 per cent was still owned by the state.[90] Secondly, the SPA selected 437 smaller-sized state-owned enterprises with up to 300 employees each. These enterprises could start self-privatization immediately. The only requirement of the SPA was that a company eligible for the 'simplified method of privatization' should select its privatization adviser from a list of private advisory agencies supplied by the SPA. The SPA entered a formal contract with each advisory agency,

89 *Hírlevél*, The State Property Agency, June 1991, Budapest, and *Világgazdaság*, 28 November 1991.
90 *Newsletter*, No.4, April 1992.

stipulating their obligations and privileges, before putting them on the list. The SPA will not be involved in actual privatizations, but may review a few cases selected at random.[91] In May 1992, a second group of 278 small and medium-sized companies was selected for the second phase of the self-privatization programme, and, in addition, 'privatization leasing' and LMBO will enhance the scope of privatization in Hungary.[92] Finally, the number of compensation claims by original owners had increased to 830,000 by May 1992. Compensation vouchers may be used for acquiring shares of state-owned companies due to be privatized, and that can contribute to faster privatization and to the more extensive involvement of Hungarians in the privatization process.

At the same time, the Hungarian parliament adopted two new laws in June 1992: one on the 'Temporarily State-Owned Property' (the property rights of which are delegated to the SPA) and another on 'Property Owned Permanently by the State and the Establishment of the State Holding Company Ltd (SHC)'. A new minister without portfolio was also appointed to supervise the SPA and the SHC. This is a negative development and indicates that the Hungarian government is reluctant to dispose of the state-owned property quickly. Instead, it enhances the state bureaucracy's involvement in exercising property rights over the state-owned assets.

In late 1992, the 'privatization minister' proposed a new technique that could accelerate privatization: government plans to introduce 'credit vouchers', available to every Hungarian citizen as a cheap loan at an interest rate much below the national bank's prime rate; maturity of the loan will be fifteen years. Each citizen is entitled to receive one voucher worth one million forints, which may be used only for acquiring state-owned property. An unlimited number of citizens may pool their vouchers to buy state-owned property; debtors are not required to take on a mortgage against the acquired property; instead, the property itself will serve as collateral security until the loan is repaid.

Another form of almost free distribution of state-owned property is a longer-term credit with an equally low interest rate but with no upper limit and with a mortgage requirement. The rationale for this

91 *Világgazdaság*, 24 October 1991.
92 See, for example, *PRIVINFO*, Vol.1, No.5.

idea is to accelerate privatization and to favour Hungarian small investors over foreigners. This, it is supposed, is the Hungarian government's way of creating an extensive middle class; however, the plan is being fiercely debated in Hungary. By early 1993, more than 1500 companies had been privatized by liquidation.[93]

In Poland, the government started large privatization with seven companies in 1990, and by the end of 1991 twenty large state-owned enterprises had been privatized centrally. In addition, another 220 enterprises went through privatization by liquidation, and the government planned to start a commercialization or liquidation of a further 800 state-owned enterprises in 1991;[94] however, after the national elections everything came to a standstill. The former Minister of Privatization, Janusz Lewandowski, elaborated a new proposal, according to which Polish state-owned enterprises could be privatized via restructuring.[95] In fact, enterprises may initiate their own privatization and sign a contract with the Ministry of Privatization. However, we must yet wait and see how far the plans outlined above will be actually realized. We must emphasize that in Poland the extremely adverse effects of the so-called 'shock therapy' substantially contributed to the very limited progress of privatization. In part, shock therapy eliminated private savings that might have been used for acquiring state-owned properties. But more significantly, a shock to the Polish economy much greater than necessary made the vast majority of the Polish enterprises immediately bankrupt and reduced their value considerably. And in early 1992, subsequent crises of the Polish government practically halted any serious effort on privatization. Privatization started to gain momentum in the second half of the year when more and more state-owned enterprises were privatized through liquidation.

In Albania, the government has managed to privatize taxi services and road transportation so far, and begun to distribute agricultural land among the rural population. However, land distribution is behind schedule and very controversial among the village population. In Romania and Bulgaria, there have been a few cases of commercialization and partial privatization of state-owned enterprises, but the actual

93 *Figyelő*, 10 December 1992; *Magyar Hírlap*, 18, 19, 23 and 27 February 1993.
94 'Privatization in Poland. Program and Achievements', op. cit.
95 'Prywatyzacja restrukturyzacyjna', *Prywatyzacja*, No.10 (13), October 1991, Warsaw, pp.1 and 8-10.

results are negligible. The position is similar in the member republics of the former USSR. In Russia, 1992 brought an increasing interest on the part of foreign investors to acquire properties. This interest is concentrated in the oil and vehicle industries, telecommunications and services. However, few actual investments have taken place so far; rather, Western advisory and privatizing agencies are visible in Russian cities, instead of industrial investors. In addition to potential foreign investments, small private businesses and private farms have been mushrooming.

Another candidate for large privatization worth mentioning is the commercial banking sector. In Hungary since 1987, and in the other East European countries since the late 1980s–early 1990s, the national banks of the countries have been decentralized and new commercial banks created from the 'monobank's' different departments. Now the number of commercial banks exceeds several dozen in Hungary and Poland, and there are more than a thousand in the former USSR. The state owns the majority share of most of these banks in the former countries, however. Foreign bankers have shown an interest in acquiring shares in commercial banks, but regulations on these deals have been fairly restrictive.

The Hungarian parliament adopted an Act on banks and banking activities in November 1991, which may open the way for a foreign capital inflow and for joint ventures with Western banks. By late 1992, the four largest commercial banks – out of about two dozen banking institutions – were prepared for partial privatization through the sale of their shares to foreign investors. The Hungarian government expects respected foreign banks to invest in Hungarian commercial banks, but the foreigners' share may not exceed 25 per cent of a bank's equity capital. A similar development can be expected in Poland and the ČSFR, with several large Western banks already present on the money markets. Obviously, the banking sector in Eastern Germany is already in West German hands. In the former USSR, several commercial banks can be regarded as private ventures, but those banks have no reserves, and they are not regulated in any way. Thus, banking is a very risky business for depositors rather than the banks themselves in the former Soviet republics.

Several East European countries have also begun to establish a stock exchange. The stock exchange began to operate in Hungary in

1990, although a few bonds had been issued by enterprises and commercial banks previously: up to now the shares of about two dozen Hungarian companies have been listed on the stock exchange. The shares of IBUSZ, Hungary's largest travel agency, were issued both in Budapest and on the Vienna stock exchange in 1990. A few other companies may follow suit with parallel issues on the domestic and foreign capital markets, and the Hungarian stock exchange may take off as thousands of compensation vouchers will be introduced and traded. In Poland, the stock exchange was set up in 1991, and at the end of 1991 the number of listed companies was eight. A stock exchange is planned in the Russian Federation as well.

We may conclude that privatization in general, and large privatization in particular, is proceeding fairly slowly, with much controversy and without a clear direction, in all East European countries. What is even more alarming than the low speed and controversial character of the process is the fact that East European governments and new political elites use privatization more and more for their own interests rather than for the benefit of the people. Governments and governing political parties want to retain a large share of the state-owned property since they consider that property to be their most valuable political and economic asset. When privatization still occurs, governments use the process to buy zealous political adherents rather than to support the emergence of a large number of free, responsible and efficient private owners. Thus, privatization is becoming a stumbling-block rather than a facilitating factor in the economic transformation in Eastern Europe. Are there other feasible ways of proceeding? Can private ownership be fostered more efficiently in order to let it take firm roots? I shall discuss these issues in the next chapter.

Appendix to Section 5.3

Let S_i denote the total number of state-owned enterprises in year i, P_i the total number of privatized companies up till year i, p_i the number of genuine privatizations, d_i the number of privatizations by splitting up (decentralizing) companies and r_i the number of companies that are added to the total number of state-owned enterprises in year i. Then,

(1)

$$S_i = S_0 - \sum_{i=0}^{n} P_i + \sum_{i=0}^{n} r_i, \text{ and } P_i = \sum_{i=0}^{n} P_i + \sum_{i=0}^{n} d_i$$

First, we want to specify the necessary and sufficient conditions for a perpetually growing share of total privatizations, P_i relative to the total number of companies in the economy $(S_i + P_i)$. Thus

(2)

$$\frac{\sum_{i=0}^{n} p_i + \sum_{i=0}^{n} d_i}{S_0 + \sum_{i=0}^{n} r_i + \sum_{i=0}^{n} d_i} < \frac{\sum_{i=0}^{n+1} p_i + \sum_{i=0}^{n+1} d_i}{S_0 + \sum_{i=0}^{n+1} r_i + \sum_{i=0}^{n+1} d_i}$$

After some rearrangements and reductions we get

(3)

$$(r_{i+1} - p_{i+1}) \cdot P_i < (d_{i+1} + p_{i+1}) \cdot S_i$$

Thus,

(4)

$$\frac{P_i}{S_i} < \frac{d_{i+1} + p_{i+1}}{r_{i+1} - p_{i+1}}$$

That is, the share of privatized companies increases if and only if the ratio of the net increment of privatized companies to the net increment of state-owned companies in year $i+1$ is larger than the ratio of private companies to state-owned companies was in year i, provided that r_{i+1} is larger than p_{i+1}. Should r_{i+1} be smaller than p_{i+1} – which is a very probable case in a sound privatization process – then the inequality relationship would have been reversed in (4).

It can easily be deduced from the inequality relations outlined above that the process of privatization has its local maximums in those years when

(5)

$$\frac{P_i}{S_i} > \frac{d_{i+1} + p_{i+1}}{r_{i+1} - p_{i+1}}$$

if $r_{i+1} > p_{i+1}$, and the inequality under (5) is reversed if $r_{i+1} < p_{i+1}$.

Private ownership will dominate the economy, that is, the share of P_i to $S_i + P_i$ will attain or exceed 50 per cent, if

(6)

$$S_0 - \sum_{i=0}^{n} d_i + \sum_{i=0}^{n} r_i < 2 \cdot \sum_{i=0}^{n} p_i$$

The inequalities described above outline the general conditions under which the privatization process will pass certain thresholds. However, there may exist special cases which deserve attention, beyond the specification of general conditions. A peculiar process of privatization may occur if $p_i = 0$ for all i, that is, if privatization takes place exclusively by splitting up companies. In that case, the number of state-owned enterprises is increased by r_i and decreased by d_i at the same time, in each year. The share of privatized companies relative to the total number of companies can still grow in this case. Specifically the share of P_i increases if

(4a)

$$\frac{P_i}{S_i + P_i} < \frac{d_{i+1}}{r_{i+1}}$$

Obviously, the privatization process has its local maximums in those years when the inequality in (4a) is reversed. The share of privatized companies to the total number of companies will be equal to or surpass 50 per cent if, by increasing the number of private companies with d_i and that of the state-owned companies by r_i in a given year i,

(6a)

$$\sum_{i=0}^{n} d_i \quad > \quad S_0 + \sum_{i=0}^{n} r_i$$

Finally, a sub-case of the peculiar way of privatization is encountered if $d_i = r_i$. This may seem a very strange way of privatizing, but it is still not a completely hypothetical one. This is exactly how the East German privatization proceeded until September 1991. Thus, companies to be privatized were first split into two parts; then one part of each enterprise was sold to private owners, while the other part remained state-owned. That is, the number of state-owned enterprises increased by exactly the same factor as the number of privatized companies. Should this process continue in the same pattern, the share of private companies relative to the total number of companies would permanently increase. However, it would never attain 50 per cent: it could only approach that threshold asymptotically.

6. Issues in Privatization and Restructuring

My intention in writing this book is to conduct a thorough analysis of privatization in Eastern Europe and to identify the decisive issues rather than to propose a new programme for privatization. Thus, this chapter aims at drawing lessons from the East European experience in the first place, and it contains only a few recommendations. However, I wish to clarify my own stand as regards the reasons for, and the direction, methods and speed of privatization. First, I shall address the issue of 'spontaneous privatization' as it occurred before and during the initial phase of the economic transformation. Secondly, I shall discuss the controversies concerning the different objectives of privatization and reasons for it in Eastern Europe. I shall show that these controversies cannot be resolved and the extremely contradictory endeavours of the governments and political elites cannot be reconciled within a comprehensive and consistent programme of privatization. Third, I shall briefly outline the impact of speed and different methods of privatization on the economic transformation. I shall focus in particular on the interrelationships between privatization and restructuring. Finally, I shall address a number of problems of privatization via the free distribution of assets. I shall argue that such distribution, when limited in extent and for a well-defined group of state-owned enterprises, can be successfully applied. However, much work still needs to be done on how free distribution of properties can be integrated in a consistent process of privatization and restructuring. I shall discuss some of these issues and present feasible methods for handling them.

6.1 FROM '*NOMENKLATURA* OWNERSHIP' TO PRIVATE OWNERSHIP VIA STATE OWNERSHIP?

I showed in the previous chapters that a peculiar form of state ownership of national assets – I called it '*nomenklatura* ownership' – was heading towards chaos in the realm of property rights in most East European countries by the late 1980s.[1] In some countries, such as Hungary and Poland, a disintegrating system of property rights has remained, by and large, within the legal framework of the socialist economy, while in other countries, such as the former USSR, *de facto* property rights have been exploited by criminal groups or by the *nomenklatura* (or both), using illegal methods. However, even in countries where legal regulation has tried to keep up with the rapid changes, enterprise managers and high-ranking officials of the state bureaucracy have succeeded in gaining considerable tangible benefits from their monopolistic position and especially their monopoly of information. The process of converting monopolistic positions into *de facto* property rights enjoyed by managers has been called 'spontaneous privatization', 'wild privatization' or '*nomenklatura* privatization' in the East European countries.

The conversion usually occurred in either of two forms. Either managers converted state-owned enterprises into joint stock companies or limited liability companies, or they founded their own private companies. In the former case, on several occasions shares of the state-owned enterprises were actually sold to outside genuine private owners as well. If a company's property rights changed hands, this meant in most cases a property sale to foreign investors, and it was almost always initiated or at least closely controlled by the state bureaucracy. It may be suspected with reason that 'sweetheart' deals

1   In his recently published book, Matolcsy – a principal architect of the new Hungarian government's economic policy and privatization plan – argued that the socialist economy was a 'self-destructing' entity. He showed that an artificially low rate of depreciation, applied to the state-owned enterprises, resulted in a high rate of enterprise profits. The bulk of those profits were taxed away by the state and transferred to the population. This 'depreciation pump' (as Matolcsy called it), along with a much higher social security tax imposed on state-owned companies than on private firms, created the basis for spontaneous privatization in Hungary, even before the political changes. Although Matolcsy's starting-point – the socialist economy as a self-destroying system – is similar to my own views, from this point of departure he arrived at a different, and I believe false, conclusion: see Matolcsy (1991).

took place between managers of the state-owned enterprises and foreign buyers which, if not illegal, were at least not exactly fair. If such deals had been uncovered, the participants could have been prosecuted under the prevailing law. (In fact, in Hungary a few privatization cases were brought to court and they were stopped by the court's decision. However, such 'show trials' created much more damage than benefit to the cause of privatization.) At the same time, it must not be forgotten that after the enterprise conversions, a vast majority of the companies' assets still remained in state hands. It is true that a part of the incomes generated within the newly detached companies ended up in the managers' and employees' wallets, and these symptoms of the economic transformation irritated people and demanded state intervention. However, the harsh political campaign launched against spontaneous privatizations was out of all proportion.

Another form of spontaneous privatization was one in which managers of state-owned enterprises started their private businesses with their own savings and exploited their monopoly on information. Managers have taken advantage of the severe shortages that have characterized every segment of the economy. On several occasions, they refused to serve their customers with goods that should have been produced by the state-owned enterprise, and instead directed customers to the 'back door' - that is, to their private company. This phenomenon has been fairly widespread in Poland since the late 1980s, and without reservation it can be called corruption. However, we can learn even from the experience of the socialist era that market competition, a liberal regime in foreign trade and liberalized prices rather than political campaigns and administrative interventions are more likely to be effective remedies against corruption. Thus, the creation of a comprehensive system and the appropriate institutions of private property rights coupled with liberalization of the economy could - and, for example, in Hungary to some extent did - serve the cause of fair privatization much more efficiently than did the fierce attacks on spontaneous privatization.

Besides spontaneous privatization, East European countries faced another and undoubtedly very important issue that needed an adequate solution: it had to be determined who the real owner of the state-owned property was and who was authorized actually to dispose of and sell that property. An obvious answer to these questions might have been that the *people* of a country owned the property and the state agencies acted as the people's agents. In that case, a logical and 'constitutional' solution would have meant that a country's parliament – as its highest legislative body – would have the authority to design the legal and institutional framework governing property rights. In addition, the parliament would be obliged to supervise the transformation of state ownership into private ownership. State agencies (as executive bodies) that were made responsible to assist and control privatization would be subordinated directly to the parliament. The Hungarian legal system of privatization, for instance, was designed along these lines in early 1990, before the free national elections. The parliament adopted some – but not all – of the necessary legal acts of property transformation between 1988 and early 1990, and it created the State Property Agency to act as an executive agent. In June 1992, the Hungarian parliament gave birth to a new government agency: the State Holding Company, which is entitled to manage the permanently-owned state assets.

After the radical political changes, the new East European governments made it their point of departure that a confused system of property rights had to be replaced by genuine state ownership first. However, they went further, arguing that since people supported those political parties that had a majority in the parliament, and governments were formed by the parties of the parliamentary majority, it must be the government rather than the parliament that is vested with the state's authority over the state-owned property. Consequently, the executive state agencies of ownership and ownership transformation were directly subordinated to, or they became an organic part of, the governments.

Arguing in favour of direct governmental rather than parliamentary control over privatization, East European governments heavily emphasized that the parliament was in no position to overview and guide privatization efficiently. They stressed that it was only the executive branch of the state that could halt spontaneous privatization as a major threat to the transition. What governments failed to mention was that by centralizing privatization the governing elite would have control over every single privatization deal and its members could use the state-owned property as well as privatization for their own political and economic benefit.

While I fully share the principle that in a post-communist economy in transition state ownership means the property rights of the people, I cannot accept the ultimate conclusion that East European governments drew from the above principle, because the conclusion does not follow from the initial assumption. East European peoples elected (or supported) deputies to represent them in parliament, rather than governments. If the transformation of property rights is considered one of the most decisive factors of the change in the economic and political system – as it should be – then the principles, strategies and methods of privatization must be elaborated and endorsed by parliament.

Theoretically, the whole of the state-owned property could be distributed equally among the population. At the first glance, this would seem to be the fairest and most consistent method of putting into practice the principle of genuine state ownership. However, as a general solution to the problem of privatization this idea can be questioned on several grounds. In the first place, the people's ownership rights are not unconstrained and unconditional. In particular, the direct distribution of state-owned enterprises among the population is unfeasible, on the grounds that it would entail complete chaos in the fields of property rights and enterprise management. Should such a distribution nevertheless occur, nobody could really exercise his or her property rights without seriously violating the property rights of others. Hence, mediating and coordinating organizations would be needed to reconcile the diverging interests of the various owners.

Different forms of an institutional ownership can be envisaged to a certain extent (I shall return to the issue of precisely what extent below), but these organizations cannot take over all state-owned properties. Should state ownership (or its equivalent, individual ownership by all citizens) be 'institutionalized' in a complete system of institutional owners as the starting-point of the East European economic transformation, this would simply mean that old forms and mechanisms of bureaucratic coordination were replaced by new types of bureaucratic coordination. Moreover, administering property rights by large institutions would entail huge coordination and transaction costs that would immediately reduce the value of the people's property.

I emphasized the time dimension or sequencing aspect of the institutional ownership because I do not deny the feasibility and economic efficiency of different forms of institutional owners in an economy where the basic institutions of private property rights have already taken firm root. (As is well known, institutional ownership accounts for the majority of ownership rights in several advanced market economies.) Neither do I think that East European countries must follow the same path of development – that is, they must repeat every small detail – that Western countries have gone through over the past two hundred years. However, some basic stages of the process of institution building cannot be by-passed without seriously risking diversion towards a distorted course of economic development.

In addition, as was discussed in Chapter 2, ownership means not only the right to use and benefit from the property but also the obligation of bearing the costs of ownership. An equal distribution of properties should also mean an equal distribution of the costs (for example, debts) that are related to those properties. However, the vast majority of the East European people are in no position to foot those bills or they are not willing to do so. Finally, an equal distribution is not necessarily an efficient distribution of property rights in the sense of Pareto optimality. In fact, it is most unlikely that free distribution of the state-owned property can be optimal in that sense. Thus, an equal distribution of the state-owned property may grant tangible benefits for a certain group of the population, while it can result in much larger losses for others. As a matter of high probability, it can also happen that even those who would derive some benefit from an equal distribution would encounter welfare losses relative to another set of property distribution which is Pareto-optimal. (To mention but one aspect: if state-owned properties are turned over to efficient private owners who make considerable profits, a sensible tax system and social policy can serve the poor much better than a piece of state-owned property which is poorly utilized.)

The above arguments do not invalidate the initial principle that state ownership means the property rights of the people. How can this principle be enforced in practice? First, the government and the other state agencies must be deprived of the actual exploitation of property rights. These bodies must be allowed to act only as agents of the people. Thus, parliament must define the rules and institutional framework of property rights. It must also overview and control the activities of the executive state agencies and the implementation of the rules of privatization. Since the rules and institutions must reflect a consensus as broad as possible among different groups of the population, the basic laws on private property rights and privatization should be adopted by a qualified majority of the parliamentary deputies (say, by 75 per cent of the votes).[2]

However, after the 'rules of the game' have been set, actual privatization can – and should – be decentralized as much as possible. In fact, actual privatization deals could be left, to a very large extent, to local governments and to private companies that specialized in conducting privatization. State agencies (especially the state property agency) would have a monitoring role and a veto right. These agencies would act as representatives of parliament. State agencies should report to parliament, and their activities as well as the privatization deals themselves must be made public. The state agencies could operate as actual sellers of the state-owned property in the case of selling nationwide monopolies or public utilities. The state should also transfer property rights to institutional owners, such as pension funds, social security and insurance funds and local governments. In addition, the state would be a participant in creating 'privatization holding companies' for a certain group of state-owned enterprises. (I shall return to this issue in the final section, below.)

Finally, incomes from the sale of state-owned properties must be used as incomes of the people. Thus, these incomes could be channelled to the reconstruction of the public infrastructure and they could contribute to the financial assets of different social funds (such as pension funds and insurance funds). The government must not be allowed to use incomes from privatization to finance the state budget deficit. Should free financial resources from property sales be left over, they could be channelled back to the private sector via loans and services created in order to support and assist private entrepreneurs.

In conclusion, I am convinced that spontaneous privatization, that is, privatization initiated by company managers or employees themselves, or by potential private buyers, could and should be a

2 See, for example, Mueller (1991).

main form of property rights transformation in Eastern Europe, provided that spontaneous privatization is preceded by the elaboration and adoption of a transparent and 'neutral' legal framework and institutional system of private property rights. (The legal framework and institutional arrangements must be neutral in the sense that they do not favour certain political or social groups.) The endorsement of an 'economic constitution' must win the support of the widest possible general consensus of the people. In this way, spontaneous privatization can and will be pursued within the rule of the law rather than by exploiting the niches of a confused legal and institutional arrangement.

6.2 THE PRIVATIZATION CONTROVERSY: WHY PRIVATIZE?

I showed in Chapter 4 that the reasons for privatization put forward on grounds of economic rationality and on the basis of careful observation of the command economy's functioning differ greatly from those that refer to so-called 'historico-ethical' and short-term political considerations. Strange as it may sound, the first group of reasons are mostly stressed by Western economists, while reasons in the second category are usually marshalled by East European politicians and their experts. Can these two groups of justification be reconciled? The answer to this question depends on the ultimate goal of the various East European countries – notably, what kind of an economic and political system they wish to create. If their aim is to return to their 'historic roots' that existed before communist rule, then the endeavours of economic rationality and those of traditionalism can be combined to some extent. Such an economic and political system, based on an authoritarian state and on a limited number of rich private owners who loyally serve the political purposes of the ruling elite, but also built on a certain economic rationality, can even prove to be viable for a while. (In this case, the East European economies' viability would presumably depend to a large extent on the magnitude of Western assistance, since economic stability would be fairly fragile and political stability also would be vulnerable).

However, if East European countries emulate the advanced Western democracies and market economies as their future model of economic and political development – and East European governments never miss an opportunity to emphasize to their Western counterparts that this is their only intention – the two groups of reasons for privatization cannot be reconciled at all. The point is that it is only the first group of reasons that points in the direction of a sound market economy with dominant private ownership and accompanying political democracy. This is not to deny that certain aspects of the past can be incorporated into a sensible and viable programme of privatization. Thus, should there be a need for it for political reasons, a symbolic compensation to people who had suffered at the hands of the communist regime for defying the law, together with a nominal amount of tangible compensation, would not interfere with privatization. However, it must be made clear to the public that the larger the amount spent on compensation the lower the efficiency of the privatization process will be (in the most favourable circumstances, no cash amount would be involved in compensation). In other words, the issue of compensation should be strictly subordinated to, and handled within, a comprehensive programme of privatization rather than considered in itself as a genuine means of privatization.

While I agree with the reasons for privatization enumerated in the first category, I find another argument to be inadequately addressed (I consider this aspect the most decisive one, at least during the period of transition). The essence of the command economies was that they could not function as self-regulated systems, but rather an immense network of political regulation was needed to keep the economies ticking over. The system of political regulation from the Politburo down to the party secretaries of enterprises, along with the whole government bureaucracy, penetrated every area and all aspects of life in Eastern Europe. Now, as new political systems are being created to replace communism, a full economic and political transformation cannot be successful until politics and the economy are disentangled. The detachment of the economy from the political sphere must go even beyond the level that is prevalent in most Western countries, in order to break up the petrified institutions and habits of a command economy. Thus, privatization is essential for Eastern Europe because this is the only way in which the economy and individual economic

6.3 THE PACE AND METHODS OF PRIVATIZATION

I share the opinion of those who emphasize that privatization must proceed as fast as possible in Eastern Europe. However, as I have shown above, the group of economists who agree on this point is very extensive. It includes János Kornai as well as Olivier Blanchard and Jeffrey Sachs. The main issue to be answered here is what is feasible when it comes to privatization? First, it must be emphasized that privatization is an extremely complex process involving the creation of an institutional and legal framework in Eastern Europe. Moreover, the process must result in actually turning over the state-owned property to private hands and in the establishment of favourable conditions for the restructuring of the economies and individual enterprises. Second, I pointed out that a clear distinction should be made, at least on the policy level, between privatization and restructuring. While privatization is aimed at redefining and reallocating property rights, restructuring should be expected to come from the new private owners and their managers in the first instance. Of course, there will still remain a non-negligible group of properties that will need government assistance in restructuring. However, government assistance must avoid administrative intervention in internal company matters – be those companies private or state-owned – and it should use market-compatible measures (such as tariffs and loans). In any case, restructuring will most probably take a much longer time than privatization itself.

When I support the cause of rapid privatization I understand this to mean that the elaboration and implementation of the legal and institutional framework of private property rights must be accomplished by the government and the parliament within a very short period of time. In other words, the redefinition of property rights and the creation of the basic institutions of private ownership cannot be piecemeal. If nothing else, the experience of earlier East European attempts at economic reform taught us that piecemeal changes in the economic institutions are bound to result in a full or partial retreat to the point of departure of the reform process. The new economic system might not be the same after the changes as it was before but it would be stuck 'in-between' and it could not surpass the threshold of an irreversible process.

Several substantial steps can be made by parliament and government within a fairly short period as regards institution building, changing regulations and creating the organizations that are supposed to assist and foster privatization. However, most of the job must be done by the subjects of privatization themselves, that is, by the companies, by private investors, by privatizing agencies, by foreign investors and by local governments, apart from a few exceptions. (Such an exception might be the group of the largest state-owned enterprises whose properties should be distributed freely to the population via privatization holdings: I shall return to this issue in the next section.) A transparent and rational system of property rights and regulations along with the adequate measures and resources of assistance to private owners will in all certainty accelerate the process of privatization. However, these changes cannot be rushed through by governments using unified – therefore fairly bureaucratic – methods.

Given the preconditions and constraints outlined above, I still believe that a clear majority (that is, more than 50 per cent) of the state-owned assets can be privatized within 4–5 years. This will still not mean that the East European countries would arrive at the 'heaven' of a Western-type market economy. Restructuring of the economies will take decades rather than years to achieve, but it can be assumed that the economies have made a good start towards an advanced market economy, and economic recession will be replaced by a recovery, followed by self-sustained economic growth.

What methods can be used or should be recommended for the East European privatization programme? I listed most of those methods in Chapter 5, and I can see no *a priori* reason to exclude any of them (with the obvious exception of any kind of restitution or compensation as a genuine method of privatization). Obviously, if actual privatization is decentralized and itself 'privatized' – that is, if it is left to private agencies and institutions – it will not be the government or any other state agency that must select the appropriate methods. Within the scope of its own resources the government may grant priority to certain methods of privatization, if it can be shown that these methods foster restructuring in a more efficient way than others. However, the government's policy and actions must be carefully controlled and endorsed by the parliament. Thus, spontaneous privatization deals or the LMBO may be appropriate for several companies while the ESOP can be used by others, or these methods can be combined in a rational way.[4]

In section 5.2 above I cited David Lipton and Jeffrey Sachs, who wrote that '... most enterprises should be privatized in a common manner to avoid debates between the government and individual enterprises.'[5] Their argument sounds sensible as long as privatization is considered as a series of deals or bargaining procedures between a government and enterprises. However, as soon as the government ceases to be a principal player in actual privatizations – as I argued it should not be – Lipton and Sachs's argument falls down. Of course, several elements of the privatization techniques may be and in fact will be common for a large number of the enterprises, since the participants of the privatization process would find those techniques efficient for their purposes. However, there would not, and should not, be a 'common manner' prescribed by the government or by other state agencies. There is one group of state-owned enterprises that does need the special attention of governments, however: the largest state enterprises. They constitute a distinct category, as has already been made clear, and I now turn to discuss the question of its privatization.

6.4 PRIVATIZATION BY FREE DISTRIBUTION: THE CASE OF THE LARGEST ENTERPRISES

When privatization began in Eastern Europe in 1989–90, it seemed obvious that the lack of sufficient demand for state-owned property would be the binding constraint on the process. Since then, potential demand – especially in the form of private savings – has somewhat increased, while supply has shrunk. Most state-owned enterprises lost value because of the collapse of the CMEA markets, and because of the companies' perpetual liquidity problems. In addition, more and more East European countries have appeared with their launch offer on the market for state-owned property; consequently, private

---

4 The most important aspects of employees' participation and its impact on a private company's productivity is excellently discussed by Levine and Tyson (1990).
5 Lipton and Sachs (1990), pp.322–3.

investors have had a wide selection to choose from. Yet despite the opposite movement of demand and supply, privatization has still proved unable to gather momentum.

After three years of economic transformation we were forced to realize that it is not merely the magnitude of demand for and supply of state-owned property that determines the success of privatization: it is rather that the structure of demand and supply must be compatible, and that the institutions of the capital market must serve as a facilitating network in the privatization process. In addition, it should also be borne in mind that economic transformation – including privatization – is an unprecedented task for the East European countries, so new and inventive methods are needed to accomplish a successful economic transition.

We discussed in Chapter 5 the proposals by prominent Western economists for an extensive free distribution of state-owned property to be made among the East European people in order to speed up privatization and restructuring. These authors supported their proposals by pointing out that actual privatizations had yielded modest results so far. Moreover, each privatization deal is surrounded by controversy and political conflict among different power groups, and the people of Eastern Europe are becoming more and more irritated by the 'spontaneous privatizations' of the old *nomenklatura*, and in general they are uninterested in privatization. In addition, Western economists emphasize that East European privatization has become a lucrative 'hunting ground' for Western investment banks and accountancy firms. These Western companies act as advisory agencies in individual cases of privatization in Eastern Europe and earn decent profits, but the results of their activities are mostly disappointing. Therefore, to overcome the pitfalls and failures of the privatization process, Western experts recommend different schemes involving free distribution.

While the diagnosis of Western economists is not completely wide of the mark – in fact, it has some relevant points although it is, by and large, fairly superficial – the remedy (and especially the recommended dosage and the 'user's instructions') are misguided. This is because, as I argued above, in all probability any 'privatization holding companies' or mutual funds created and controlled by East European governments would reinforce state intervention. Thus, privatization would result in the political selection of private owners and managers rather than widespread and democratic forms of private ownership. In addition, East European countries lack those hundreds (or thousands) of skilled managers who could act as experts in corporate governance. In general, East European countries are incapable of absorbing a large number of sophisticated corporate governance and investment banking institutions in the short run. Thus, a vast network of institutional owners, as the main form of privatization created by governments (with Western assistance), would become a 'plastic Wall Street' - to borrow Kornai's expression - rather than organic institutions of privatization.

However, free distribution via privatization holdings (or mutual funds) as one method among others - and only where it is appropriate - is not an inconceivable and unviable idea. Western investment banks and firms of accountants are not the 'devil's advocates'. In fact, Western private advising agencies serve the cause of privatization in Eastern Europe poorly because they are asked - indeed, required - to do so. Western private agencies can certainly be blamed for not warning East European governments about the consequences of their own assistance to an ill-designed privatization process. In addition, the expertise and advice of Western investment banks might be used in a far more appropriate fashion in Eastern Europe. However, it is the task of the East European parliaments and governments to establish the necessary and suitable conditions for Western agencies' participation in privatization and restructuring.

There is a group of state-owned enterprises in each East European country that requires privatization methods different from those employed for the bulk of the state-owned property. This group consists of a few dozen of the largest state-owned enterprises which are extremely difficult to decentralize and restructure in a sensible way, and which have not attracted a substantial amount of foreign direct investment. (There is no precise measure for this 'substantial amount', but it seems reasonable that foreign investment is not substantial enough if it does not secure at least a relative majority ownership for the foreign owner in the company.) Obviously, the number of the largest companies that may belong to this group can differ country by country: in all probability, the group will be bigger in the largest republics of the former USSR than in smaller East

European countries. Moreover, the size of the group will vary inversely with the country's development level and the extent of its progress in privatization so far. In addition, the list of the enterprises that are included in the group may change even during the process of setting up the privatization holding companies, since the list will be finalized by the private holdings themselves.[6] (Moreover, the list would be shortened if a state-owned enterprise found a private buyer or had already made progress in the process of self-privatization.)

Privatization with free distribution would start with the government proposing a list of the largest state-owned enterprises and calling for tenders from domestic and foreign private companies (including banks) to create privatization holding companies. Private domestic and foreign companies would be allowed – they should even be encouraged – to submit joint proposals, since the privatization holding companies would need manifold expertise and skills. Joint ventures between domestic and foreign companies could be given well-defined preferences in the evaluation of the tenders.

Along with the tendering procedure the government should design a plan for the free distribution of shares in the privatization holding companies among the adult population (rather than a direct distribution of the enterprises' shares). This plan should be as simple and clear as possible, and it should as far as possible avoid political considerations and any distinction between different groups in the population. The government should use international organizations as expert advisers in designing the privatization plan. (In addition, the government should search for the least expensive solutions as regards the preparatory phase and the phase of implementation.) Finally, both the call for tenders and the free distribution plan must be submitted to parliament and endorsed by it.

The evaluation of the bid offers should be made by an independent

6   It is worth reminding ourselves of the fact that 'picking out' a group of the largest enterprises and imposing direct control over them was a regular practice of the communist governments in the past: this happened, for instance, in Hungary in 1971-72. The aim of such government actions was, above all, to regain control over investments and nationwide imbalances in general. However, the privatization method that I propose is different in essence from the method of 'picking out' exercised by the Hungarian government. In particular, the government (and parliament) would be involved in the initial phase of the process and they would supervise the legal aspects of privatization, but from then on the private holding company would act in a completely autonomous way, independent of the government.

body formed from representatives of international organizations (such as the World Bank, the European Bank for Reconstruction and Development, the European Communities, etc.). The government should have a strict minority representation in the selection body at most. After a selection has been made, the state-owned enterprises that remained on the list should be allocated among the privatization holdings, on the basis of the free distribution plan elaborated by the government and experts from the various international organizations. (This means that a rough preliminary evaluation of the enterprises' assets and market values is unavoidable in order to achieve a more or less equal distribution of the enterprises among the privatization holding companies.)

The privatization holding companies would receive their authorization from parliament, but from that moment on they would act as fully autonomous private companies. Parliament – in practice, its executive agent, the state property agency – could monitor and control the privatization holding companies only within the legal framework of privatization that had been enacted by parliament. Thus, the state property agency could interfere if the prevailing laws were violated by the privatization holding company, but it could do so only by using the existing legal procedures.

The privatization holding companies could act as *de facto* owners of the state-owned enterprises, with a few limitations. Thus, they would be free to close down companies or parts of the enterprises, they could reorganize the enterprises, divest capital from an enterprise and invest it in others. The privatization holding companies could also establish new companies or acquire shares in other companies than those in their portfolio. However, it seems sensible to impose some restrictions on the privatization holding companies as regards the sale of complete enterprises.

A frequently voiced argument against the privatization holding companies is that they would be tempted to sell the enterprises as soon as possible and for a price well below the realistic market values. In that case, privatization holding companies would gain a decent amount of profit for doing almost nothing but disposing of their assets. However, this view is based on a misunderstanding. After all, the privatization holding companies do not own the assets, since their securities would be entirely in the hands of the population.

Should the price of the shares increase, the dividends from that increase would belong to the ultimate owners of the shares, namely the population. (Obviously, the revenues of the privatization holding would also grow in proportion to its successful operation.) On the other hand, should the price of the shares decline, the privatization holding company would also lose, and the shareholders would try to sell the less attractive shares. The only safeguard needed against the privatization holding companies' malpractices is that they should not be allowed to transform the assets into their own incomes.

Another serious concern of several East European economists is that most people would immediately sell their shares and spend the incomes from those sales on consumer goods. Thus, inflation would get a large boost from free distribution and, in addition, the price of the shares would plunge. As regards the inflationary impact of a possible mass sale of the freely distributed shares, this cannot be denied. However, the danger should not be exaggerated either, since, if the programme of free distribution is well prepared and explained to the people, and the whole process of creating the privatization holding companies commands confidence, then there is every reason to believe that a considerable part of the population will consider his or her shares acquired in this manner to be a sensible savings option. In particular, if the domestic currency were to become convertible or a part of the dividends of the privatization holdings were to be paid in convertible currencies, then the privatization shares could compete effectively with hard currency private bank accounts or state bonds.[7] There may still be a sizeable group of people who want to convert their easily earned 'gift' into consumption, and this will undoubtedly have an inflationary impact. However, the total value of enterprise assets concerned would be only a fraction of the population's annual expenditure on consumption – the ratio of the enterprise assets to personal consumption would remain below ten per cent in all certainty – and only another fraction of this asset value would be converted into actual consumption. Thus, the inflationary impact of selling freely distributed shares would be negligible.

Finally, there has been extensive discussion in the literature about

---

7 For instance, in Hungary, the private savings in hard currencies doubled between mid-1990 and mid-1991. In addition, there is a growing interest in state bonds and some other securities on the part of a substantial group of the Hungarian population.

whether the free distribution of shares should be instituted via the stock market, or by using the existing and, it is hoped, rapidly developing banking sector. There can be arguments for and against both options. In countries such as Hungary and Poland, where a stock market already exists, it may be more sensible to introduce the shares of the privatization holdings on to the stock market. Against that, though, it may take some time before the whole population becomes acquainted with the rules and functioning of a stock market, although of course the privatization holding companies will be able to trade their shares. As evidence shows, more and more brokerage agencies are starting to operate in these countries as well, and the shareholders can buy the services of those private companies. In other countries, where the financial market is in its embryonic stage, it is more sensible to use the services of the banking sector.

I should emphasize strongly that, however great the significance I attached to the establishment and operation of the privatization holding companies, they will still remain only one of the 'players' in the privatization process. It is not excluded – and I find it even desirable – that the privatization holding companies will become the seeds of an extensive system of institutional owners. But in Eastern Europe such a system can develop only gradually and over a fairly long time-scale. Realistically, the number of privatization holdings should not exceed five in countries such as Hungary, whereas it can be between five and ten in Poland, and not many more in the Russian Federation or Ukraine. (There may be a need for more than ten privatization holding companies in Russia, but there the constraints of expertise and management skills and the country's absorption capacity are strictly binding.)

It must be made clear that the free distribution of state-owned property is not presented as the best and most efficient way of privatization in general, but is a 'second best solution' in the special circumstances of Eastern Europe. If there is a group of state-owned enterprises that cannot be privatized and restructured in an 'easy' way, and at the same time this group consists of enterprises that are decisive actors among East European industries, but the management and restructuring of these companies should not be left to governments, then a programme of free distribution involving privatization holding companies may be the most feasible solution to the problem of privatizing and restructuring those enterprises. Thus, free distribution can and should be conducted by following the rules of economic rationality. In addition, free distribution is also a matter of political decision by the freely elected parliaments, an act that would convince people that ultimately they are in fact the owners of the state's assets. Moreover, so far in the East European countries, privatization has occurred exclusively as the concern of state bureaucracies, enterprise managers and foreign investors; as something that should not actively concern the population at large, although it is the people who must face and endure most of the consequences of privatization (namely, the closing down of enterprises, unemployment and growing inequalities among different groups of the population). Thus, most people have become at best indifferent to privatization, or they have been irritated by the dirty business practices and feel elbowed out again, as they had been under the communist regime. Consequently, a carefully prepared programme of free distribution might help to regain people's trust and restore the new parliaments' and governments' fading credibility.

In addition to the free distribution via privatization holding companies, the parliament could allocate a relatively small share of the state-owned assets to private pension funds, social security and insurance funds. For instance, when a state-owned enterprise is sold to private buyers, a minority share of its assets or the revenues from the sale could be compulsorily turned over to the institutional owners mentioned above. In parallel with this process, the financing obligations of the state budget towards the social security system could be reduced. This would, of course, need a comprehensive reform of the state finances, but that is one of the most crucial aspects of the economic transformation in any case, since so long as state expenditures exceed 50 or even 60 per cent of the annual GDP in the East European countries – and most of these expenditures are financed by the government by imposing extremely high taxes on the enterprises – the economy remains on the track of self-destruction. Such a form of financing the state means, in practice, that enterprises must convert their assets into revenue flows in order to survive. Hence, privatization must proceed along with the contraction of the state sector not only in the enterprise sphere but in the governmental sphere as well.

Evidence also shows that privatization itself has been unable to reverse the chronic recession in the East European economies. Demand for state-owned properties is insufficient and it is at least as restrained as the propensity to invest on the part of private investors. There are signs that private entrepreneurs favour new investments for acquiring run-down state-owned property, in which case privatization should progress hand in hand with an improvement in the economic conditions for new private investments.

7. Concluding Remarks

Privatization in Eastern Europe is the biggest challenge of our times, both intellectually and in practical terms. In this book I have tried to address the most important issues of privatization in Eastern Europe, but I readily admit that numerous questions have not even been raised and a great number of problems have not been fully tackled. Since East European privatizations will remain a main subject for analysis and discussion for several years – even decades – to come, I do not see this study as a conclusion but rather a point of departure in the analysis.

I discussed several principles and practices of privatization as they have surfaced in different East European countries. I must admit that I am more familiar with the Hungarian case than with, say, the case of Bulgaria or the former USSR, but I am convinced that the main issues and problems that have been presented in this book are relevant for all East European countries. I am fully aware of the fact that these countries differ greatly as regards their level of economic development, their past attempts at economic reforms and their accomplishments in that respect, and their progress in economic transformation. For that very reason, I do not believe that universal methods of privatization can and should be recommended to each and all of them. In fact, I am convinced, for instance, that the decades of experimenting with economic reforms in Hungary provided that country with a substantial advantage over most of the others when it began economic transformation – despite the fact that the Hungarian reforms yielded modest visible results during the communist era and each individual reform measure was extremely controversial in its time. Consequently, it may well be true that several East European countries cannot avoid an initial phase of economic reforms – perhaps less ambivalent than the Hungarian reforms were – before a full liberalization and privatization of the economy can be successfully accomplished.

For instance, in the case of Russia and the other CIS countries Western analysts strongly argued that the old system of the state bureaucracy and regulation must not be demolished until the economy was stabilized and put on the track of economic transformation. I accept that for a short period far more extensive and powerful central control is needed over the economy in the CIS countries, or in Romania, for instance, than in Hungary, Poland or the ČSFR. The length of this period would depend on the time needed to create a new government bureaucracy within democractic institutions. In that case, it seems obvious that there is little choice but to use the existing state bureaucracy. It should be stressed that even during the transition period, existing bureaucracies can be used for tackling the immediate operative tasks, such as avoiding a complete break-down of the transport system or averting natural disasters. However, at the same time, every possible effort must be made to subordinate state bureaucracies to democratically elected institutions and to circum-scribe the authority of the executive branches of the state by a democratically adopted constitution. In addition, the autonomy of the enterprises must be extended in parallel with the liberalization of markets, prices and foreign trade, and with the liberalization of the rules governing private enterprise. No time should be wasted as regards privatization initiated by the enterprises, enterprise managers and employees themselves. And as the disintegration of the former Soviet Union proceeds, and new independent countries emerge from the member republics, a more differentiated and less centralized approach may become feasible to privatization in those countries as well.

All in all, the Soviet-type economic system was imposed upon the East European countries over four decades ago. Now as these countries have embarked on economic transformation, they can each learn from the positive achievements, as well as from the mistakes, of the others. What they should not do is repeat the old practice of trying to implement identical institutions and using the same tools in order to build capitalism, as they did when they started building communism.

Bibliography

Akerlof, George, A., Andrew K. Rose, Janet L. Yellen and Helga Hessenius (1991), 'East Germany in from the Cold: The Economic Aftermath of Currency Union', *Brookings Papers on Economic Activity,* No.1, Washington, DC, pp.1-104.

Alchian, Armen A. and Harold Demsetz (1973), 'The Property Rights Paradigm', *Journal of Economic History,* Vol.33, No.17 (March).

Antal, László (1985), *Gazdaságirányítási és pénzügyi rendszerünk a reform útján* (The Hungarian System of Economic Management and Monetary System on the Road to Reform), Budapest: Közgazdasági és Jogi.

Åslund, Anders (1989), *Gorbachev's Struggle for Economic Reform,* Ithaca, NY: Cornell University Press.

— (1991a), 'Principles of Privatization for Formerly Socialist Countries', Working Paper No.18, Stockholm Institute of Soviet and East European Economics.

— (1991b), 'Principles of Privatization', in László Csaba (ed.), *Systemic Change and Stabilization in Eastern Europe,* Aldershot: Dartmouth.

— and Örjan Sjöberg (1991), 'Privatization and Transition to Market Economy in Albania', Working Paper No.27, Stockholm Institute of Soviet and East European Economics.

Bauer, Tamás (1981), *Tervgazdaság, beruházás, ciklusok* (Planned Economy, Investments, Cycles), Budapest: Közgazdasági és Jogi.

— (1984) 'The Second Economic Reform and Ownership Relations', *East European Economics,* Vol.22 (Spring-Summer), pp.33-47.

Beksiak, Janusz and Jan Winiecki (eds) (1990), *The Polish Transformation: Programme and Progress,* London: Centre for Research into Communist Economies.

Berliner, Joseph S. (1957), *Factory and Manager in the USSR,* Cambridge, MA: Harvard University Press.

Bishop, Matthew and John Kay (1988), *Does Privatization Work? Lessons from the UK,* London: Centre for Business Strategy, London Business School.

Blanchard, Olivier, Rudiger Dornbusch, Paul Krugman, Richard Layard and Lawrence Summers (1991), *Reform in Eastern Europe,* Cambridge, MA: MIT Press.

Blue Ribbon Commission (1992), *Sustainable Forint Convertibility for Hungary: What Type, and When and How to Introduce It?* Policy Study No.1 of the Joint Hungarian-International Blue Ribbon Commission, Indianapolis and Budapest: Hudson Institute and BRC Hungarian Foundation, June 1992.

Borensztein, Eduardo and Manmohan S. Kumar (1991), 'Proposals for Privatization in Eastern Europe', *IMF Staff Papers*, Vol.38, No.2 (June), pp.300-326.

Brennan, Geoffrey and James M. Buchanan (1985), *The Reason of Rules: Constitutional Political Economy*, Cambridge: Cambridge University Press.

Brown, Stuart S. and Carlos M. Asilis (1991), 'Efficiency and Stability of Decentralized versus Centrally Arbitrated Regional Reform in the Soviet Union', Working Paper No.24, Stockholm Institute of Soviet and East European Economics.

Brus, Wlodzimierz (1972), *The Market in a Socialist Economy*, London and Boston: Routledge & Kegan Paul.

Bujak, Zbigniew (1991), *Przepraszam za Solidarność* (I apologize for Solidarity), Warsaw: BGW.

Comisso, Ellen (1991), 'Property Rights, Liberalism, and the Transition from "Actually Existing" Socialism', *East European Politics and Societies*, Vol.5, No.1 (Winter), pp.162-88.

Dabrowski, Marek (1991), 'Privatization in Poland', *Communist Economies and Economic Transformation*, Vol.3, No.3, pp.317-25.

Dallago, Bruno (1992), *Accounting for CPEs in Transition: System-Related Issues in Measuring Economic Performance – Measurement of the Private Sector's Contribution: Final Report*, Washington, DC: World Bank.

Dembinski, Pawel H. (1991), *The Logic of the Planned Economy*, Oxford: Clarendon Press.

Ellerman, David P., Ales Vahcic and Tea Petrin (1991), 'Privatization Controversies East and West', *Communist Economies and Economic Transformation*, Vol.3, No.3, pp.283-98.

Eörsi, Gyula (1968), *A gazdaságirányítás új rendszerére áttérés jogáról* (On the Legal Framework of the Transition to a New System of Economic Management), Budapest: Közgazdasági és Jogi.

Filatotchev, Igor, Trevor Buck and Mike Wright (1992), 'Privatization and Buy-outs in the USSR', *Soviet Studies*, Vol.44, No.2, pp.265-82.

Fisher, Irwing (1923), *Elementary Principles of Economics*, New York: Macmillan.

Frydman, Roman, Andrzej Rapaczynski and John S. Earle (1993a), *The Privatization Process in Central Europe*, CEU Privatization Reports, Vol.1, London: Central European University Press.

— (1993b), *The Privatization Process in the Republics of the Former Soviet Union*, CEU Privatization Reports, Vol.2, London: Central European University Press.

Furubotn, E. and S. Pejovich (1974), *The Economics of Property Rights*, Cambridge: Ballinger.

Gintsburg, L.Ya. and Ye.B. Pashukanis (1935), *Kurs sovetskogo khozyaistvennogo prava*, Moscow: Gosudarstvennoe izdatel'stvo Sovetskogo zakonodatel'stva.

Goldmann, Josef, and Karel Kouba (1967), *Hospodářský růst v ČSSR* (Economic Growth in the ČSSR), Prague: Československé Akademie Věd.

Grigoriev, Leonid (1991), 'Ulterior Property Rights and Privatization: Even God Cannot Change the Past', Working Paper No.32, Stockholm Institute of Soviet and East European Economics.

Grosfeld, Irena (1990), 'Prospects for Privatization in Poland', *European Economy*, No.43 (March), pp.139-50.

Grossman, Gregory (1983), 'The Party as Manager and Entrepreneur', in G. Guroff and F. V. Carstensen (eds), *Entrepreneurship in Imperial Russia and the Soviet Union*, Princeton, NJ: Princeton University Press.

Hanson, Philip (1990), 'Property Rights in the New Phase of Reforms', *Soviet Economy*, Vol.6, No.2, pp. 95-124.

Hare, Paul and Irena Grosfeld (1991), 'Privatization in Hungary, Poland and Czechoslovakia', Discussion Paper No.544 (April), London: Centre for Economic Policy Research.

Hayek, Friedrich von (1944), *The Road to Serfdom*, Chicago, IL: University of Chicago Press.

Hewett, Ed A. (1988), *Reforming the Soviet Economy*, Washington, DC: Brookings.

Hodjera, Zoran (1991), 'Privatization in Eastern Europe: Problems and Issues', *Communist Economies and Economic Transformation*, Vol.3, No.3, pp.269-81.

Horvat, Branko (1991), 'Reprivatization or Something Else?', *Communist Economies and Economic Transformation*, Vol.3, No.3, pp.367-74.

Jackson, Marvin (1990), 'The Privatization Scorecard for Eastern Europe', *RFE Report on Eastern Europe*, 14 December, pp.23-31.

— (1991), 'The Progress of Privatization', *RFE Report on Eastern Europe*, 2 August, pp.40-45.

Janackova, Stanislava and Kamil Janacek (1992), 'Privatization Strategy in International Comparison', *Prague Economic Papers*, Vol.I, No.1, pp.73-84.

Johnson, Paul M. (1989), *Redesigning the Communist Economy: The Politics of Economic Reform in Eastern Europe*, Boulder, CO: East European Monographs.

Joint Economic Committee of the Congress of the United States (1989), *Pressures for Reform in the East European Economies, Vols 1 and 2*, Washington, DC: Government Printing Office.

Jones, Leroy, P. (1990), *Selling Public Enterprises: A Cost–Benefit Methodology*, Cambridge, MA: MIT Press.

Kawalec, Stefan (1989), 'Privatization of the Polish Economy', *Communist Economies*, Vol.1, No.3, pp.241-56.

Khanin, Grigorii I. (1991), *Dinamika ekonomicheskogo razvitiya SSSR*, Novosibirsk: Nauka.

Klacek, Jan *et al.* (1992), 'Economic Reform in Czechoslovakia (Current Evaluation)', *Prague Economic Papers*, Vol.I, No.1, pp.5-28.

Kluson, Václav (1992), 'Alternative Methods of Privatization', *Prague Economic Papers*, Vol.I, No.1, pp.55-72.

Kornai, János (1959), *Overcentralization in Economic Administration*, London: Oxford University Press.

— (1980), *The Economics of Shortage, Vols A and B*, Amsterdam: North Holland.

— (1986), 'The Hungarian Reform Process: Visions, Hopes and Reality', *The Journal of Economic Literature*, Vol.24, No.4, pp.1687-1737.

— (1990), *The Road to a Free Economy? Shifting From a Socialist System: The Example of Hungary*, New York: Norton.

— (1991), 'A privatizáció elvei Kelet-Európában' (The Principles of Privatization in Eastern Europe), *Közgazdasági Szemle,* Vol. XXXVIII, No.11, pp.1021–40.

Laban, Raul and Holger C. Wolf (1991), 'Wholesale Privatization and the Waiting Option: A Political Economy Model', MIT paper presented at the sixth annual congress of the European Economic Association, 31 August.

Levine, David, I. and Laura D'Adrea Tyson (1990), 'Participation, Productivity, and the Firm's Environment', in Alan S. Blinder (ed.), *Paying for Productivity: A Look at the Evidence,* Washington, DC: Brookings.

Lewandowski, Janusz and Jan Szomburg (1989), 'Property Reform as a Basis for Social and Economic Reform', *Communist Economies,* Vol.1, No.3, pp.257–68.

Lindbeck, Assar (1973), 'Ekonomiska system - ett mångdimensionellt fenomen', *Ekonomisk Debatt,* Vol.1, No.1, pp.3–18.

Lipton, David and Jeffrey Sachs (1990), 'Privatization in Eastern Europe: The Case of Poland', *Brookings Papers on Economic Activity,* No.2, pp.293–341.

Liska, Tibor (1985), *Koncepció és kritika* (Conception and Critique), edited by István Siklaky, Budapest: Magvetö.

Major, Iván (1991a), *Why the Communist Economies Collapsed* (manuscript), Washington, DC, and Stockholm.

— (1991b), 'Privatization in Hungary: Principles and Practices' Working Paper, No.20, Stockholm Institute of Soviet and East European Economics.

— (1991c), 'The Hungarian Economy in Transition: Some Aspects of Stabilisation, Liberalisation and Privatisation', Working Paper No.23, Stockholm Institute of Soviet and East European Economics.

— (1991d), 'Private and Public Infrastructure in Eastern Europe' *Oxford Review of Economic Policy,* Vol.7, No.4, pp.76–92.

Martin, Peter (1991a), 'Privatization Stirs Controversy', *RFE Report on Eastern Europe,* 4 October, pp.6–9.

— (1991b), 'Foreign Joint Ventures on the Rise', *RFE Report on Eastern Europe,* 22 November, pp.6–12.

Matolcsy, György (1991), *Lábadozásunk évei. A magyar privatizáció. Trendek, tények, privatizációs példák* (The Years of Convalescence: The Hungarian Privatization: Trends, Facts and Examples), Budapest: Privatizációs Kutatóintézet.

Michalski, Jacek (1991), 'The Privatization Process in Poland: The Legal Aspects', *Communist Economies and Economic Transformation,* Vol.3, No.3, pp.327–36.

Mises, Ludwig von (1935), 'Economic Calculation in the Socialist Commonwealth', in Friedrich von Hayek (ed.), *Collectivist Economic Planning,* London: Routledge & Kegan Paul, pp.87–130.

Montemartini, Giovanni (1967), 'The Fundamental Principles of a Pure Theory of Public Finance', in Richard A. Musgrave and Alan T. Peacock (eds), *Classics in the Theory of Public Finance,* New York: St Martin's.

Mroz, Bogdan (1991), 'Poland's Economy in Transition to Private Ownership', *Soviet Studies,* Vol.43, No.4, pp.677–88.

Mueller, Dennis C. (1991), 'Choosing a Constitution in Eastern Europe: Lessons from Public Choice', *Journal of Comparative Economics,* Vol.15, No.2 (June), pp.325–48.

Murrell, Peter and Mancur Olson (1991), 'The Devolution of Centrally Planned Economies', *Journal of Comparative Economics,* Vol.15, No.2 (June), pp.239-65.

Newbery, David M. (1991), 'Reform in Hungary: Sequencing and Privatization', *European Economic Review,* Vol.35, pp.571-80.

North, Douglas, C. (1981), *Structure and Change in Economic History,* New York and London: Norton.

— and Robert Paul Thomas (1973), *The Rise of the Western World* (New Economic History series), Cambridge: Cambridge University Press.

OECD (1991), *Accounting Reform in Central and Eastern Europe,* Paris: OECD.

Okolicsanyi, Karoly (1991), 'The Compensation Law: Attempting to Correct Past Mistakes', *Radio Free Europe Report on Eastern Europe,* May 10, pp.7-11.

Pejovich, Svetozar (1990), *The Economics of Property Rights: Towards a Theory of Comparative Systems,* Dordrecht: Kluwer.

Pelikan, Pavel (1990), 'Evolution of Structures, Schumpeter Efficiency, and a Limit to Socialist Economic Reforms', Working Paper No.2, Stockholm Institute of Soviet and East European Economics.

Roland, Gérard and Thierry Verdier (1991), 'Privatization in Eastern Europe: Irreversibility and Critical Mass Effects', Discussion paper No.9105 (June), Centre d'Economie Mathématique et d'Econométrie.

Sachs, Jeffrey (1989), 'Introduction', in *Developing Country Debt and the World Economy,* Chicago: University of Chicago Press, pp.1-32.

— (1990), 'What Is to Be Done?', *The Economist,* 13 January.

Sappington, David (1987), 'Privatization, Information and Incentives', Cambridge: National Bureau of Economic Research.

Sárközy, Tamás (1981), *A szocialista vállalatelmélet jogtudományi alapjaihoz* (On the Legal Basis of the Socialist Theory of Enterprise), Budapest: Közgazdasági és Jogi.

— (1986), *Egy gazdasági szervezeti reform sodrában, 1984–1985.* (On the Course of an Economic-Organizational Reform, 1984-1985), Budapest: Magvetô.

Schrettl, Wolfram (1992), 'Transition with Insurance: German Unification Reconsidered', *Oxford Review of Economic Policy,* Vol.8, No.1, pp.144-55.

Shapiro, Carl and D. Robert Willig (1990), 'Economic Rationales for the Scope of Privatization', Discussion Paper No.41, Princeton University.

Šík, Ota (1967), *Plan and Market Under Socialism,* White Plains, NY: International Arts and Sciences Press.

Slider, Darrell (1991), 'Embattled Entrepreneurs: Soviet Cooperatives in an Unreformed Society', *Soviet Studies,* Vol.43, No.5, pp.797-821.

Soós, Attila K. (1984), 'A Propos the Explanation of Shortage Phenomena: Volume of Demand and Structural Inelasticity', *Acta Oeconomica,* Vol.33, Nos 3-4, pp.305-20.

— (1986a), *Terv, kampány, pénz* (Plan, Campaign, Money), Budapest: Kossuth and Közgazdasági és Jogi.

— (1986b), 'Informal Pressures, Mobilization and Campaigns in the Management of Centrally Planned Economies', Working Paper No.86/246, European University Institute, Florence.

— (1990), 'Privatization, Dogma-Free Self-Management, and Ownership', *East European Economics,* Vol.28 (Summer), pp.53-70.

Stark, David (1990), 'Privatization in Hungary: From Plan to Market or From Plan to Clan?', *East European Politics and Societies*, Vol.4, No.3 (Fall), pp.351-92.

Szalai, Erzsébet (1990), *Gazdasági mechanizmus, reformtörekvések és nagyvállalati érdekek* (Economic Mechanism, Strivings for Reform and the Interests of the Large Enterprises), Budapest: Közgazdasági és Jogi.

— (1991), 'Integration of Special Interests in the Hungarian Economy: The Struggle between Large Companies and the Party and State Bureaucracy', *Journal of Comparative Economics*, Vol.15, No.2 (June), pp.284-303.

Tardos, Márton (1972), 'A gazdasági verseny hazánkban' (Economic Competition in Hungary), *Közgazdasági Szemle*, Nos 7-8 (July-August), pp.911-27.

Tóth, István J. (1991), 'A spontán privatizáció mint kormányzati politika', *Külgazdaság*, No.9, pp.35-52.

UN ECE (1992), 'On Property Rights and Privatization in the Transition Economies', in *Economic Survey of Europe 1991-1992*, Geneva: UN Economic Commission for Europe, May.

Venediktov, L. (1950), *A Szovjetúnió vállalatainak szervezete és jogi helyzete* (Organization and Legal Status of the Enterprises in the USSR), Budapest: Szikra.

Vickers, John and George Yarrow (1988), *Privatization: An Economic Analysis*, Cambridge, MA: MIT Press.

Vogelsang, Ingo (1990), *Public Enterprise in Monopolistic and Oligopolistic Industries*, Chur, London, New York and Melbourne: Harwood Academic Publishers.

Voszka, Éva (1984), *Érdek és kölcsönös függöség* (Interests and Mutual Dependence), Budapest: Közgazdasági és Jogi.

— (1990), *Hármasút* (Triple Crossroads: the Role of Government Committees in Central Decision-Making), Budapest: Pénzügykutató Rt.

— (1991a), 'A 'spontaneitástól' a 'központosításig' és tovább. (A kormányzat szerepe a privatizációban)' (From Spontaneity to Centralization and Beyond: The Government's Role in Privatization), *Külgazdaság*, No.1, pp.19-34.

— (1991b), 'Homályból homályba. A tulajdonosi szerkezet a nagyiparban' (From Dusk to Dusk: Ownership Structure in Large-scale Industry), *Társadalmi Szemle*, No.5, pp.3-12.

— (1991c), 'Tulajdonosi szerkezet - tulajdonosi érdek' (Ownership Structure - Owners' Interests), *Közgazdasági Szemle*, No.9, pp.860-71.

Wicksell, Knut (1967), 'A New Principle of Just Taxation', in Richard A. Musgrave and Alan T. Peacock (eds), *Classics in the Theory of Public Finance*, New York: St Martin's.

Wiles, Peter (1982), 'Are There Any Communist Economic Cycles?', *The Aces Bulletin*, Vol.XXIV, No.2 (Summer), pp.1-20.

Winiecki, Jan (1990), 'No Capitalism Minus Capitalists', *Financial Times*, 20 June.

Index